NEW DIRECTIONS FOR MENTAL

H. Richard Lamb, *University of Southern California*
EDITOR-IN-CHIEF

Managed Mental Health Care

William Goldman
U.S. Behavioral Health

Saul Feldman
U.S. Behavioral Health

EDITORS

Number 59, Fall 1993

JOSSEY-BASS PUBLISHERS
San Francisco

MANAGED MENTAL HEALTH CARE
William Goldman, Saul Feldman (eds.)
New Directions for Mental Health Services, no. 59
H. Richard Lamb, Editor-in-Chief

Microfilm copies of issues and articles are available in 16mm and 35mm, as well as microfiche in 105mm, through University Microfilms Inc., 300 North Zeeb Road, Ann Arbor, Michigan 48106.

LC 87-646993   ISSN 0193-9416   ISBN 1-55542-676-X

NEW DIRECTIONS FOR MENTAL HEALTH SERVICES is part of The Jossey-Bass Social and Behavioral Science Series and is published quarterly by Jossey-Bass Inc., Publishers (publication number USPS 493-910).

EDITORIAL CORRESPONDENCE should be sent to the Editor-in-Chief, H. Richard Lamb, Department of Psychiatry and the Behavioral Sciences, U.S.C. School of Medicine, 1934 Hospital Place, Los Angeles, California 90033.

Cover photograph by Wernher Krutein/PHOTOVAULT © 1990.

 The paper used in this journal is acid-free and meets the strictest guidelines in the United States for recycled paper (50 percent recycled waste, including 10 percent post-consumer waste). Manufactured in the United States of America.

CONTENTS

EDITORS' NOTES

In barely a half dozen years, managed mental health care has become a major presence in the medical industrial complex, exerting a significant influence on the way mental health and substance abuse services are provided. By whatever name—managed care, managed competition, utilization review, prospective payment, or capitation—and in whatever form, it is growing rapidly, gathering momentum, changing practice patterns, and stimulating change.

By and large, the entities responsible for these developments are specialized managed behavioral health organizations, for-profit, freestanding, or owned by insurance carriers and health care conglomerates. Creatures of the 1980s, they arose as a response to the economic imperatives of spiraling unmanaged mental health and substance abuse costs. Due primarily to the explosive growth of private, for-profit psychiatric hospitals and their aggressive marketing practices, payors reacted. In light of escalating costs, payors were essentially faced with two alternatives—cut benefits (which many have done) or manage them so as to control costs and ensure quality.

Mental health is the last of the major health specialties to be exposed to managed care, with its emphasis on accountability and systematic oversight. Providers see *managed care* as a euphemism for restricting care, while managed care organizations and payors see this approach as a means of maintaining benefits and providing more care at less cost.

Well-established utilization review practices have been in place for over a decade for medical-surgical insured health benefits. Building on this experience, specialty mental health managed care firms developed the next generation of case management–based managed care. The lists below elaborate some of the contrasts between traditional utilization review and mental health case management.

Non-Network-Based Utilization Review

- Unknown providers (clinicians and facilities)
- Providers resistant to managed care
- Increased feelings of confusion and resentment by insured
- Preauthorization requests, often after non-emergency hospitalization

The editors wish to express their great appreciation to Elisabeth Gruskin for her assistance and editorial effort in bringing this volume together.

- Patients admitted to more regressive levels of care (inappropriately restrictive and expensive)
- Patients at greater risk of paying retroactively for disallowed services
- Increased appeals
- Less financial savings
- No control of quality
- Little or no treatment planning or continuity of care, therefore greater chance of recidivism

Network-Based Case Management

- Employee education and management consultation before implementation
- Face-to-face assessment
- Case managers are mental health experts
- Individualized treatment plans, not diagnosis driven
- Substitution of benefits
- Treatment plan review at least every three days for inpatients; at least every seven days for residential; as appropriate for outpatient levels of care
- Ability to divert from inappropriate levels of care
- Benefit protection and control
- Inpatient and outpatient expertise
- Outreach for clients who drop out of treatment
- Aftercare follow-up for substance abuse
- Continuity of case management in long-term treatment
- Prospective and concurrent rather than retrospective review
- Focus on level and quality of care versus focus on level only in utilization review
- Ability to shape practice patterns using referral system
- Potential to enhance benefits through benefit design and consultation

But where does managed mental health go next? It is not atypical, particularly in health care, for such questions to be asked even about programs and processes that are relatively new. In Chapter One, Mary Jane England and Veronica V. Goff suggest that the organized care system—one that includes health and mental health with continuous quality improvement and care management teams—should be the model of the future.

Chapters Two through Six describe different models of managed care; for example, in Chapter Two, Leon Wanerman describes a model of managed care for children and adolescents that in his judgment improves quality and controls costs. Given the number of studies that suggest a high rate of inappropriate child and adolescent admissions to inpatient facilities, any promising alternative deserves serious consideration.

But managed mental health services may also have an important effect on medical costs. There is already evidence to suggest that mental health services have an "offset" effect—that is, they can reduce the cost of more expensive medical services. Michael S. Pallak, Nicholas A. Cummings, Herbert Dörken, and Curtis J. Henke suggest in their Hawaii Medicaid study—detailed in Chapter Three—that managed mental health services bring about greater medical cost savings than unmanaged services. In Chapter Four, Bentson H. McFarland, Robert A. George, David A. Pollack, and Richard H. Angell describe the Oregon model that would provide health services for all poor and uninsured people in the state according to a list of priorities including mental health and substance abuse. Health and mental health services would be integrated and paid for on a capitated basis.

In their description of Alcan Aluminum Corporation in Chapter Five, Laura Altman and Wendy Price illustrate how one company turned to managed care as a solution and developed a new benefit structure. David Dangerfield, in Chapter Six, describes a similar process under way in Utah, as the state tries to cope with the rising costs of mental health services for Medicaid enrollees.

Managed care's intrusion into the sanctum of fee-for-service office and hospital practice has provoked controversy that is now only beginning to abate. Chapters Seven through Nine provide different perspectives on the impact of managed care. In Chapter Seven, Doyle Carson describes how one psychiatric hospital is developing a new managed care culture and coping with staff resistance to briefer hospital stays and alternatives to inpatient care. From another perspective, that of community mental health centers, Charles Ray and Monica Oss—in Chapter Eight—wonder and worry about the role of the centers in the new managed care environment and suggest that it has great potential for them.

Substance abuse services have also contributed to the large behavioral health cost increases. As Claire V. Wilson suggests in Chapter Nine, the twenty-eight-day-inpatient-stay model, which until recently had been the standard treatment of (provider) choice for substance abuse, is much less common under managed care, since hospitals and other providers are required to justify and modify their treatment practices.

Whatever form it may take, it is clear that managed mental health care will continue to grow and change. If we are to achieve universal coverage and rational use of resources in a planned system of care, then to the extent possible, the changes that take place should be guided by research and experience—that is, by a literature. This volume is an attempt to contribute to that literature by bringing together the extensive experience and expertise of people who are working in and developing managed mental health care in a variety of forms. We are grateful to them.

Saul Feldman
William Goldman
Editors

SAUL FELDMAN, D.P.A., is chair of U.S. Behavioral Health, a subsidiary of the Travelers, in Emeryville, California. Earlier, he was an HMO executive, head of the nation's community mental health programs, and director of the Staff College at the National Institute of Mental Health. He is the founder and editor of the Journal of Administration and Policy in Mental Health.

WILLIAM GOLDMAN, M.D., is senior vice president for medical affairs and medical director at U.S. Behavioral Health, and clinical professor of psychiatry at the University of California, San Francisco. Earlier, he was director of an urban community mental health center, director of a city mental health system, a state mental health commissioner, and an HMO medical director.

Corporate America views the initial phase of health reform in the United States as government-stimulated, competing organized systems of care utilizing some of the managed care principles and designs already in place.

Health Reform and Organized Systems of Care

Mary Jane England, Veronica V. Goff

The organized systems of care approach is a work in progress in which all health services are provided by competing systems (Cronin, 1992). It evolves from experience in both the public and private sectors. The aim is to make high-quality, necessary health care available to all Americans at an affordable cost. Several leading employers are now working with providers to define, build, and assess organized systems of care. Managed mental health organizations in place, as distinct from just utilization review programs, already practice many if not all of the OSC principles presented here.

Organized Systems of Care

An organized system of care (OSC) is an integrated financing and delivery system that uses a panel of multidisciplinary providers selected on the basis of quality and cost management criteria. It incorporates continuous quality improvement and incentives to provide only appropriate and necessary care, and it is accountable to patients and purchasers for quality, cost, and outcome criteria. The concept of organized systems of care reflects a vision of the future American health care system. While some elements of this vision exist today, it is a working concept toward which health care and mental health care reform efforts must be directed.

In an OSC, arbitrary benefit limits are not necessary. Treatment is based on individual need determined by patient choice, medical necessity, severity of illness, and level of functioning. Services are aimed at maximizing functional capacity. Those who need intensive care are able to get it; those who do not are moved to less intensive levels of care. Standardized clinical and functional assessments are used to establish health status and inform treatment practices.

Cost Increases and Shifting

Mental health costs have been among the fastest growing of all specialties (Towers, Perrin Employee Benefits Information Center, 1989). Between 1986 and 1990, for example, employer costs for mental health and substance abuse services increased by an average of 50 percent. The most generous benefit plans were those that experienced the most dramatic increases.

In the face of rising and seemingly unmanageable costs, many payors are restricting their employee mental health benefits. Common restrictions include arbitrary caps on annual and lifetime dollars and days, along with greater cost sharing by beneficiaries. Unfortunately, such restrictions leave the most seriously ill without adequate protection. Restrictions often prove futile for payors as well—employers report consequences such as diagnosis gaming, overuse of general medical care, and higher disability costs.

Restrictions also result in a two-tier mental health system. The private sector primarily serves the insured; hospitalization and office-based outpatient therapy are the predominant settings. The uninsured, poor, and severely ill are served primarily in the public system, characterized by people with severe and chronic disorders and underfunded community-based services. Though often more versatile, public services are increasingly in short supply.

Within both sectors, services are fragmented. Particularly in the private sector, services reflect little understanding of the long-term needs of mental and substance abuse disorders. Treatment often consists of symptom reduction for an active episode. The absence of continuing care or long-term case management makes it difficult to prevent relapse or hospital readmission.

While the public sector has shown itself to be more adept at defining systems of care for the chronically ill, lack of funding and poor integration between human service agencies have prevented smooth coordination of medical, mental health, and other human services.

Poor Benefit Design and Inappropriate Care

Treatment of mental and substance abuse disorders is most often determined by the available benefits. Private insurance, for example, commonly reimburses more generously for inpatient services, thus creating a financial incentive to hospitalize. Though this practice was originally designed as a way to protect those most in need of treatment, the disparity in coverage between inpatient and outpatient care discourages early intervention and encourages the inappropriate overuse of hospitals. A study by the National Center for Health Services Research found that 45 percent of all substance abuse hospitalizations between 1980 and 1985 could have been managed in outpatient settings (Hewitt Associates, 1989). A number of other studies on the care of children and adolescents have shown similar results.

Gross overuse of hospitalization has continued to drive up the mental health and substance abuse costs of private insurers. Inpatient charges for adolescents grew by 65 percent between 1986 and 1988 (Frank, Salkever, and Sharfstein, 1991). Although care in less intensive settings is more broadly available, employers still spend an average of 70 percent of their mental health dollars on hospital-based services (Broskowski, 1990).

Explosive growth in the supply of psychiatric beds has also been a factor. Between 1984 and 1990, the number of freestanding psychiatric and substance abuse hospitals increased by 84 percent (Kim, 1990). The beds were filled through sophisticated marketing campaigns targeting adolescents and substance abusers, resulting in many unjustified and even harmful hospitalizations as well as sharply increased costs.

Poor Recognition and Treatment

Most people with a diagnosable mental disorder do not seek treatment; those who do usually see a primary care physician. But mental health and substance abuse disorders are often unrecognized or inappropriately treated in the primary care setting. For example, a 1989 Rand Corporation study found that primary care physicians in a fee-for-service setting detected depression in only 51 percent of patients with a current diagnosable depressive disorder (Wells and others, 1989).

Early recognition, accurate diagnosis, and appropriate management or referral would result in lower spending by reducing the number of unnecessary physician visits and the inappropriate use of tests and medication for the somatic symptoms of undiagnosed mental disorders. However, improved skills in recognition, treatment, and referral are not the only issues. System-based incentives are needed to improve the link between primary care and mental health/substance abuse providers and increase the knowledge of primary care physicians in diagnosis, referral, management, and follow-up of patients.

Basic Principles for Reform

Mental and substance abuse disorders can be prevented or treated effectively if identified early and treated quickly. Routine early identification with appropriate treatment may in fact dramatically reduce the use of general medical services. In contrast, if undiagnosed and untreated, these disorders often prove seriously disabling and costly to individuals, families, and society as a whole.

Reform of the American health care system should include universal access to a full continuum of medically necessary and appropriate mental health and substance abuse services, comparable to those provided for physical illness. The services available should include preventive, primary, acute, rehabilitative, and chronic care and be provided in a way that flexibly meets individual needs. Just as in medical-surgical care, services should be provided according to generally accepted standards of practice with meaningful documentation of value received from treatment, including functional outcome measures. An ongoing evaluation of system effectiveness and treatment outcomes should be established and maintained to determine such standards. To both improve the quality of care and contain costs, those services can only be provided through organized systems of care.

Distinctions from Current Managed Care

Organized systems of care differ from current managed care efforts that emphasize mainly utilization review in several respects: (1) the quality of care is based on an understanding of the needs and expectations of consumers and payors; (2) the specification and improvement of the service is continual and measurable; and (3) everyone in the system is involved in improvement because everything can be improved.

These principles suggest that the care will differ from community to community based on need, information on resource use, and costs. Outcomes of care will be used to assess the value of the care provided, and external utilization review will be brought in-house. Utilization review now is essentially an inspection system focused on poor performance. In contrast, OSCs are designed to continually improve quality, not simply penalize outliers.

System Characteristics

Organized systems of care would represent a fundamental change in the way mental health and substance abuse services are provided. While some health plans incorporate several OSC elements, the concept has not yet been implemented in the truest sense. In an OSC, barrier-free access to care is available through a primary care physician, a mental health professional, or an employee assistance counselor available through employment. The problem of unrecognized disorders is resolved through a triage mechanism performed by mental health and substance abuse professionals in coordination with primary care physicians. In this way, patients get the most appropriate level of care. The triage system is supported by an array of incentives.

The OSC delivers care through care management that integrates the physical, psychological, and administrative needs of the patient. Primary care physicians, allied health professionals, and mental health professionals form a team, with one team member identified as responsible for overseeing the care for each individual.

Focused care management is the goal. Treatment can be individualized and flexible, with comprehensive services available. A care manager is available for all at-risk patients using inpatient, partial hospitalization, or residential services. The use of a care manager also might be triggered by outpatient utilization exceeding a predetermined amount. The care manager coordinates with the primary provider to ensure an ongoing postdischarge treatment regimen. As appropriate, the care manager also coordinates with available workplace programs, such as health promotion, employee assistance, disability management, and workers' compensation.

To enhance prevention and early intervention, employee assistance–type programs are provided. The referral aspect of these programs recognizes that people generally do not know about the myriad of choices they have for mental health and substance abuse services and would be well served by professional assistance (Koepke, 1991).

The services provided by an OSC include the full continuum of care—prevention, early intervention and referral, screening, diagnosis, acute care, and rehabilitation—in a wide spectrum of settings from hospitalization to home, for all age groups.

Current Demonstrations of Evolving OSCs

Two examples illustrate the ways in which OSCs are developing.

Honeywell. By 1993, Honeywell will have approximately twelve thousand domestic employees enrolled in organized mental health systems (McDonald, 1992). One system is now working and a second is under development. In a given community, Honeywell works with one multidisciplinary group practice for all mental health and substance abuse care. The goal is a long-term, mutually supportive partnership with continuous quality-of-care principles central to the process. The group practice is responsible for creating a system that offers a full continuum of services through a multidisciplinary panel of providers. Ideally, the system uses salaried providers so that there is no incentive to over- or undertreat. In addition, the system must define a continuing quality-of-improvement process, including provisions for ongoing outcomes evaluation based on clearly defined standards of care.

The OSC has a strong prevention focus, with an employee assistance program to provide early and easy access to services and integration with occupational programs such as health promotion, drug testing, and disability management.

The system determines the most appropriate care and develops a treatment plan. Multidisciplinary evaluation, treatment, and follow-up are available as appropriate. Although a treatment plan may include diverse levels and modes of care over time, one member of the care team is responsible for tracking the patient through the various treatment settings. The patient and family are fully informed so that the care plan is known to everyone.

The advantages to both Honeywell and the provider organization include the ability to deliver the highest level of appropriate care versus treat-

ment controlled by restrictive benefit design; cost containment through quality and variation control versus denial of care or discounted fees; and an ongoing relationship that allows for the development of a common language
and purpose, consistent messages to beneficiaries, and shared feedback to
continually improve the system.

Digital Equipment Corporation. Another innovative effort is under
way at Digital Equipment Corporation. Digital has committed itself to working with its HMOs to improve health care (Angel, 1992). To that end, HMO
standards for data, financial stability, access, quality, and mental health and
substance abuse care have been developed.

With regard to mental health and substance abuse services, some of the
problems identified by Digital and its HMOs include rigid adherence to benefit limits, inadequate case management, barriers to initial access, lack of
specialty staff, and no documentation of value received by patients.
Expectations for improvement in these areas have been developed, with an
emphasis on increasing flexibility to meet the needs of patients and more
data to help inform the process.

For example, a triage mechanism has been defined to improve access to
the most appropriate level of care in the system. An individualized treatment
approach is encouraged, with decisions based on determinations of medical
necessity and measurement of patient functional status and well-being. Case
management is recommended for all inpatient and alternative treatment fa-
cility admissions to ensure an appropriate postdischarge regimen and continuity of care.

One of the most exciting initiatives involves an intensive evaluation of
treatment for depression at three of the HMOs offered to Digital employees.
This effort developed out of Digital's participation in the Outcomes
Management Consortium sponsored by the Managed Mental Healthcare
Association. (In 1989, the Managed Mental Healthcare Association was created by approximately 150 employers interested in ensuring that their employees were receiving the best quality care for their health care dollars.)

Outcomes Research

The OSC model will be advanced through work such as that now under way
on outcomes at the University of Arkansas. The aim is to "improve mental
health care by utilizing disorder-specific outcome modules which can be part
of routine clinical care" (Smith, 1992, p. 1).

Outcome modules have been developed or are under development for
five disorders: major depression/dysthymia, panic disorder, alcohol abuse/
dependence, schizophrenia, and drug abuse. Each of the modules has seven
phases of development: conceptual work, development of a module, field and
validity testing of the prototype module, revision of the module, feasibility
testing in clinical settings, formal testing of the module in a quality improve-

ment program, and its use in a quality improvement program to improve the quality of care. The module that is furthest along in the process, depression/dysthymia, is undergoing feasibility testing in the Digital/HMO effort mentioned above, as well as in a community mental health center.

Transition to Organized Systems of Care

Organized systems of mental health and substance abuse care can best achieve both cost management and quality improvement by integrating all health services. Health Insurance Purchasing Cooperatives (HIPCs) would be established as the new major purchasers negotiating with competing OSCs on a regional basis. The HIPCs would be inclusive, enroll the employed and unemployed, and represent the vehicles for university coverage. As the transition proceeds, it is important that several questions affecting basic assumptions about appropriateness and equity in mental health care be considered. Among them are the following: How can the medical cost–offset effect of early and appropriate mental health treatment be measured? As access to mental health care increases, can it bring about a direct reduction in medical spending? Can accountability in mental health treatment be imposed without narrowly defining disorders as biologically determined? How can the care system include such vitally needed nonmedical services as respite care and support groups?

By applying the key attributes of OSC—use of a multidisciplinary panel of providers selected on quality and cost management criteria and the delivery of a full continuum of services, from prevention and primary care through chronic care—and incorporating the principles of continuous quality improvement, quality health care at an affordable cost can be achieved.

References

Angel, K. "Behavioral Healthcare Tomorrow." Paper presented at the second annual conference of the Institute for Behavioral Healthcare, Chicago, Sept. 1992.

Broskowski, A. "Current Mental Health Care Environments: Why Managed Care Is Necessary." APA Professional, 1990, 21 (55), 39.

Cronin, C., and Milgate, K. "Organized Systems of Care: A Vision of a Future Healthcare Delivery System." Paper presented to the Washington Business Group on Health, Washington, D.C., May 1993.

Frank R. G., Salkever, D. S., and Sharfstein, S. S. "A New Look at Rising Mental Health Insurance Costs." Health Affairs, 1991, 10 (2), 116–123.

Hewitt Associates. Managing Health Care Costs. Lincolnshire, Ill.: Hewitt Associates, 1989.

Kim, H. "Sicker Psych Patients Could Help Hospitals." Modern Healthcare, Apr. 23, 1990.

Koepke, M. Treatment Options for Alcohol Abuse: Information for Health Care Purchasers. Quality Resource Center Research Report. Washington, D.C.: Washington Business Group on Health, 1991.

McDonald, B. "Building Systems of Care." Paper presented at the National Leadership Conference on Mental Health: Quality and Science in Corporate Practice, sponsored by the National Institute of Mental Health and the Washington Business Group on Health, Washington, D.C., Sept. 1992.

Smith, G. R. *Mental Health Outcomes Project.* Project summary. Little Rock: Department of Psychiatry and Behavioral Sciences, University of Arkansas for Medical Sciences, and the VA HSR&D Field Program for Mental Health, 1992.

Towers, Perrin Employee Benefits Information Center. *Psychiatric and Substance Abuse Cost Survey.* Valhalla, N.Y.: Towers, Perrin Employee Benefits Information Center, 1989.

Wells, K. B., Hays, R. D., Burnam, A., Roger, W., Greenfield, S., and Ware, J. E. "Detection of Depressive Disorder for Patients Receiving Prepaid or Fee-for-Service Care." *Journal of the American Medical Association,* 1989, 262 (23), 3298–3302.

MARY JANE ENGLAND, M.D., *is president of the Washington Business Group on Health, national program director of the Robert Wood Johnson Foundation's Mental Health Services Program for Youth, and a member of the executive committee of the White House Health Project.*

VERONICA V. GOFF, M.S., *is manager of mental health promotion for the Washington Business Group on Health and director of the D/ART National Worksite Program.*

Managed Mental Health for Children and Adolescents

Leon Wanerman

At their wit's end, the family of a sixteen-year-old female called U.S. Behavioral Health (USBH), their managed care company, for authorization to send their daughter to a residential treatment center for adolescent substance abusers. They told the USBH care manager that their daughter had been drinking heavily and using marijuana frequently for over a year. She was failing in school and defiant at home, refused to comply with family rules, stayed out until all hours, and often returned home drunk. She had already had several brushes with the police for disorderly behavior, refused to discuss her situation with her parents or teachers, and denied that she had a problem. Unsure where to turn, the parents had been referred to a friend of a friend who allegedly knew something about teenage substance abuse treatment. He had recommended a residential treatment center hundreds of miles away that he said had helped several other teenagers.

After a lengthy discussion with the father, it became clear to the care manager that the parents were not able to provide sufficient structure and supervision for their daughter and that a highly structured treatment program would be needed, at least at the outset. The care manager did not, however, think that a residential treatment center so far away was the best plan. In the local community, there was an adolescent day treatment center with a strong substance abuse component. The parents agreed to give this program a try and to be responsible for getting their daughter to and from the center each day.

The care manager authorized an evaluation by the day treatment center staff, who agreed that the young woman was appropriate for them. An initial eight-hour-per-day, five-day-per-week treatment was authorized. By the end of the first week, the daughter had made a reasonably good connection with the program staff, and the family was actively involved in family therapy and education. These were seen as essential elements in the treatment and could not have occurred in any comparable way at the remote residential center.

The care manager's involvement had led to a treatment plan that was clinically sound and cost-effective. Following the initial authorization, an additional three weeks of day treatment were certified in weekly increments, followed by one year in the center's aftercare program.

As this case shows, the starting point of any approach to the treatment of disturbed children and adolescents is not particularly different in managed from that in nonmanaged care. In either situation, a sound clinical evaluation and treatment plan are required as well as a recognition that treatment of children and adolescents is more complex than that of most adults. This has to do with the child's fundamentally greater dependence on an environmental support system and the participation of that system in the treatment process. An effective managed care program must ensure a standard of care that encompasses this perspective.

In virtually every case, the parent or parent surrogates should be involved. Often, siblings, grandparents, and other family members may be as well. Active contact is often required with teachers and other school personnel and is sometimes necessary with representatives of social service, juvenile justice, and general health care agencies. It is essential that the treating clinician and the care manager have a basic understanding of this complexity in the treatment of child and adolescent patients. It shapes decisions about who is to be involved in the evaluation and individually tailored treatment.

Managed Care Perspective

Other factors should affect the care manager's approach to the treatment plan. These are not generally a high priority for the private practitioner and all too often are barely considered, yet they are vital for effective treatment planning.

The care manager has immediate, on-line access to information about the patient's mental health or chemical dependency benefits, including benefit limits, treatment modalities covered, annual and lifetime dollar maximums, any limits on treatment units (for example, outpatient sessions per year or inpatient days per year), deductibles, and the like. Information on how flexibly the benefits can be used—such as whether the benefits for inpatient care can be used for alternatives such as partial hospitalization or outpatient treatment—is also included.

This information, combined with the clinical data, allows for comprehensive treatment planning. It helps the care manager consider the available financial resources as part of the overall management of the case and leads to a treatment plan of optimal quality, from both a clinical and a cost point of view.

The managed care perspective is also influenced by other factors, such as the importance of least restrictive care, the desired intensity of treatment, and the need to formulate a trajectory of care across a broad continuum of services. *Restrictiveness of care* refers to the level of treatment a patient may be in at any particular time. It is commonly understood to encompass a range from outpatient (least restrictive) to treatment on a locked hospital ward (most restrictive). Other levels—such as partial hospitalization, residential treatment, and open hospital units—are in the intermediate positions on this continuum.

Intensity of treatment refers to who is being seen, how often, and in what modalities. While it is often believed that intensity and restrictiveness of treatment are directly proportional, this is not necessarily true. A state hospital ward, for example, is restrictive, yet it is low in intensity. Conversely, outpatient treatment including weekly individual therapy, family therapy, and participation in one or more substance abuse groups would be high on an intensity scale but low in restrictiveness.

The good care manager is concerned about the *trajectory of care*—that is, anticipating the entire episode of care over time and planning treatment across a continuum of restrictiveness and intensity. The perspective of the care manager should encompass the clinical picture, benefits, concern about restrictiveness and intensity of care, and anticipation of the course of treatment over time. This point of view leads to highly focused, complex questions: What level of care is needed to ensure safety or to prevent significant risk? What intensity of treatment is required to bring about effective and timely change? When might the restrictiveness and intensity change, and what should the next balance be? Do the available resources permit the needed care now, and will they permit the anticipated course of treatment? If not, what alternatives are available and acceptable?

These and other questions should lead to the development of focused, concrete goals for the initial phase of treatment as well as for the entire episode of care. Such goals should be developed for the child, the parents, and other significant persons in the child's life. This type of focused treatment planning should also include regular reviews by the treating clinician and the care manager together, focusing on progress made toward the agreed-on treatment goals and any necessary modifications.

The following case examples illustrate the work of a care manager in helping the treating clinician to identify and adopt the dominant treatment goals at a particular time. The first case illustrates the setting of primary goals at the onset of care. The second shows the importance of shifting to a new goal at the crucial point of resuming an interrupted treatment. Both illustrate the role of the care manager as the colleague of the clinician in treatment planning.

The evaluation of a thirteen-year-old boy revealed a seriously disturbed youngster with a disorganized and bizarre thought process. His strange and troublesome behavior exacted an enormous toll on his parents, who were tired of the need for constant vigilance. In his own attempt to make sense of the world, the child became preoccupied with learning all the public transportation routes in his city. He spent endless time traveling on subways, buses, and streetcars. Exasperated, his parents decided to allow him free rein, but a number of incidents occurred during his travels that were potentially dangerous. His mounting fear led to his devising increasingly bizarre and grandiose schemes that he inappropriately believed would protect him. In fact, this effort to make greater order and sense of the world led to even greater disorganization.

The above information was reported by the evaluating clinician, whose proposed treatment plan included an evaluation of the need for medication and psychotherapy aimed at improved reality testing, strengthening more adaptive defenses, and decreasing instances of disorganized thinking and behavior. The care manager agreed with the plan but felt that for it to succeed, the boy would have to be stabilized and kept safe. This would require an immediate intervention with the parents to help them limit his dangerous travels by placing him in a safe and structured after-school environment. This interposition of an immediate and crucial goal helped get the longer-range treatment off on the right footing. Without it, the subsequent treatment might have floundered.

A seven-year-old girl resumed treatment after an interruption of several months. Initially, she had been referred for extreme defiance and impulsiveness. She had begun to tyrannize her parents, who were recent immigrants. In their homeland, much of her care had been given over to servants. Forced by political conditions to leave their country, the parents had found resettlement extremely difficult. They had lost economic status and comforts, relationships with important people, and their home. They were ill-prepared to deal with the many practical obstacles they faced. Their daughter had also lost a great deal: the regularity of her life, friends, a beloved pet, and the protection of adults who were competent to care for her.

The clinician and the care manager agreed that the initial goal of treatment for the patient would be greater ability to control her impulses. This would depend, in large part, on the reestablishment of order in her life and on her working through her grief about the many losses. The goals for her parents were to create more order in their daughter's life, to be more effective and consistent in setting appropriate limits, and to acknowledge her grief.

The first months of the initial therapy with the child went well, but the therapist found it much more difficult to help the parents. In frustration, the therapist suggested that they might benefit from therapy themselves and suggested a referral for each of them. The father was particularly offended by this suggestion, with its implication that he was disturbed, and abruptly terminated the child's therapy after four months.

Even more disruptive behavior at home and at school led them, three months later, to request that the daughter's therapy be resumed. The treatment goals were assumed to be a continuation of those previously established. The sessions with the child, however, were different from the earlier ones. She destroyed toys, seemed unable to play in a sustained way, and was often sadistic and provocative. She seemed bent on hurting herself and the therapist. During the next review with the care manager, the therapist indicated her bewilderment at this new behavior. The care manager suggested that perhaps a different goal was in order at this stage in the treatment. The focus needed to shift to the patient's anger at the therapist for her failure to protect the prior treatment relationship from disruption by the father. When this was addressed, the destructive behavior stopped and was replaced by sadness echoing some of the child's previous losses. The recognition that a new focus was needed at a particular moment in the treatment brought about a return to an effective course.

Focused Adolescent and Child Treatment

The concepts just described can be implemented in diverse ways. Different managed care companies have organized their approach to child and adolescent services in varying ways. The USBH model is described below.

In 1990, the leadership of USBH decided to develop a dedicated child and adolescent team to manage the care of all patients under the age of nineteen. This decision followed from the repeated observation that, while the existing cadre of care managers were experienced in mental health and chemical dependency treatment, there were not enough care managers with expertise in treating children and adolescents. Even though the care managers had direct access to and consulted regularly with the deputy medical director—a senior child psychiatrist—the management of the child and adolescent cases was too inconsistent.

Formation of the new Focused Adolescent and Child Treatment (FACT) team began in early 1991 with the hiring of the first dedicated child/adolescent care manager. By late 1992, the team consisted of two supervisors and seven care managers, accounting for about 25 percent of the total cases and 40 percent of the twenty-four-hour care days being authorized at any given time. All of the FACT care managers are licensed and highly experienced, with an average of over ten years' experience in all aspects of child mental health and chemical dependency services. Among them are former directors of psychiatric hospital inpatient programs and outpatient agencies. Others have served in staff and supervisory positions in residential treatment and day treatment programs. Most have small ongoing private practices.

Even before the development of the FACT team, efforts were undertaken to expand the number of child/adolescent specialists within the USBH network of contracted clinicians and facilities. Of the over 20,000 contracted clinicians in the USBH nationwide network, approximately 18 percent have child/adolescent specialty training and experience. Fifteen percent of the over 1,400 contracted facilities have dedicated specialty child or adolescent services.

Typically, the first point of contact with USBH by someone seeking help for a child is a call from a parent. The call is answered by one of our intake

coordinators, all of whom are at least master's-level mental health professionals. At least one is "on-line" seven days a week, twenty-four hours a day. The
intake coordinator obtains enough clinical information to determine the nature of the problem and the degree of urgency. Via on-line information in the
computer, a clinician specialized to work with children will be identified,
often in the family's immediate geographic area. A referral will be made to
this provider, and between one and five outpatient visits for a thorough evaluation will be authorized. When the evaluation has been completed, a written report is sent by the clinician for review by a FACT care manager. When
there is some urgency, the care manager is called by the clinician, and immediate treatment planning is done.

There are two child psychiatrists on the permanent staff who are actively
involved in the supervision of the FACT team. Each of them has over twenty-
five years of clinical and administrative experience in a wide range of areas,
including private practice, teaching, community mental health, and various
inpatient, outpatient, and partial care programs for children and adolescents.

All hospital and residential treatment cases are reviewed regularly with
one of the child psychiatrists; the same is done for aftercare treatment of all
discharged patients for a minimum of two months postdischarge. In addition, the psychiatrists are available on a continual, daily basis to the FACT
care managers. The psychiatrists meet weekly with the entire team for a case
conference as well as with the team supervisors to discuss other aspects of
the caseload, the work of the care managers, and administrative matters. An
example of their joint efforts is the planning for a pilot in-home mental
health services project.

The continual supervision of the care managers by the team supervisors
and the child psychiatrists is viewed as a central element in ensuring quality
of care. It allows for individualized case planning rather than rigid, formula-
driven approaches. The constant availability of on-site, immediate supervision
leads to continual refinement of decision-making criteria that can be utilized
flexibly and are regularly reviewed and modified. Examples of criteria for
level-of-care decision making are given in the appendix to this chapter.

The following two cases illustrate the functions of the USBH FACT care
managers. The first portrays the care manager's ability to arrange high-quality
care while avoiding the disruption and cost of unnecessary hospitalization;
the second demonstrates clinical continuity, bridging services in a variety of
settings and coordinating care among different clinicians and facilities.

A call is received from the mother of a ten-year-old-boy who informs the intake
coordinator that the child's pediatrician has recommended psychiatric hospitalization. The call is transferred immediately to one of the FACT team care managers. The care manager learns that the boy has been increasingly withdrawn and
sad at home. He is normally easygoing, but now he bursts into tears easily with
little apparent reason. His teachers have also noted a gradual withdrawal from

peer interactions and a drop in his usually high academic performance. On the previous day, his teacher had called the mother and told her that the boy said that he wished he were dead. The distraught mother called the family pediatrician, who suggested immediate hospitalization. The boy had not made any attempt to harm himself and told his mother that he was "only kidding" about wanting to die.

The care manager suggested an immediate evaluation to determine whether hospitalization was necessary or whether an alternative treatment approach might be indicated. The parents agreed to this approach, and the care manager arranged an appointment with a network child specialist for later that same day. The clinician saw the boy and the parents that evening. She determined that there was no acute suicidal risk and that the youngster's symptoms were primarily a reflection of considerable turmoil within the family concerning a recent change in the father's employment resulting in his having to travel a great deal. The change had resulted in angry bickering between the parents about the father's unavailability to the family; the bickering had confused and frightened the boy.

The clinician did not think hospitalization was needed. She and the care manager agreed that a family therapy–oriented crisis intervention was the appropriate plan. The family was seen three to four times a week for the next three weeks, at which point the situation was sufficiently stable to permit continuing outpatient therapy once a week. Not only was the hospitalization clinically unnecessary, it would have further disrupted the child and the family's life and could even have made matters worse. It also would have risked exhausting the limited annual or lifetime mental health benefit, leaving little or no resources for when they might be truly needed.

The charge nurse at a general hospital intensive care unit (ICU) requests authorization to transfer a seventeen-year-old male to the hospital's psychiatric ward. No psychiatric evaluation had yet been done. The care manager arranged for a network psychiatrist to go to the ICU and evaluate the need for psychiatric inpatient care.

The psychiatrist learned that the young man had been brought to the hospital by the police forty-eight hours earlier, after he had lacerated both of his arms and nearly bled to death. He was described as severely depressed; he knew that he had tried to kill himself, but had some memory gaps about the actual events. He wanted to die and expressed the clear intention to kill himself by any means available as soon as possible. He was medically stable. The psychiatrist recommended immediate transfer to the psychiatric ward and agreed to follow the patient. The care manager initially authorized three hospital days.

On review three days later, the following information was obtained: the patient spent the first twelve years of his life in a cult where he had witnessed, been a victim of, and participated in repeated acts of sadistic physical, sexual, and ritual abuse. At age twelve, he ran away, was picked up by the authorities, spent several years in a variety of foster homes, and was finally adopted by one of the foster families. He had been a marginal and erratic student but was about to graduate from high school at the end of the school term. He suffered from night-mares and frequent flashbacks and had often mutilated himself with safety pins and other sharp objects, though this was his first suicide attempt. It appeared to have been precipitated by an argument with his adoptive father, who had told him he would "never amount to anything" and that the family "would be glad to get rid of him at the end of the school year." He remembered being panicked at this thought and wanting to kill his father, but his memories about the attempt to kill himself were fuzzy. The adoptive parents were interviewed and were exasper-ated by how little they had gotten back from all they felt they had invested in this boy. They were willing to get him whatever help he might need but wanted him out of their lives as much as possible.

It was clear to the care manager and her supervisors that treatment for this young man would be long and complex. Fortunately, the father's insurance pro-vided fairly extensive coverage. The care manager began immediate planning to achieve maximum treatment from the available benefits. She anticipated that after treatment in an acute care hospital, the young man might need additional twenty-four-hour care in a subacute residential treatment center. Following that, a day treatment program combined with a halfway house or a supervised apart-ment setting and ongoing outpatient psychotherapy would likely be necessary. She began to consider which of these services could be covered under the insur-ance benefit and which might come under available public programs. There were no residential treatment programs in the local community, so that phase of treatment would involve a geographic move and a change of treatment person-nel. The care manager would thus be the common thread linking the various components and clinicians who would be involved in the young man's long-term care.

Conclusion

The preceding cases illustrate how a managed care approach can work to the benefit of children and adolescents through a collegial relationship be-tween care manager and provider. They also demonstrate that, done prop-erly, managed care can bring about high-quality treatment while reducing inappropriate hospital utilization and controlling costs. Perhaps most im-portant, this approach can protect generally limited and restrictive mental health benefits so that they are available for those situations in which care is truly needed.

Appendix

U.S. Behavioral Health Guidelines for Level-of-Care
Decisions in Mental Health Care for Children and Adolescents

Degree of Impairment: Severe

Severe disturbance in one or more of the following: affect, behavior, thought processes, and judgment, such that

Client's basic survival needs cannot be provided independent of a twenty-four-hour structured therapeutic environment; and

Client is experiencing significant interference in familial, educational, and other age-appropriate functions due to the severity of the symptoms; and

Client's history and developmental abilities indicate that he or she is capable of greater age-appropriate functioning and is assessed to be likely to show improvement with therapeutic interventions; and/or

Client is unable to exhibit adequate age-appropriate behavioral control

and

Actual or imminent risk of suicide and/or harm to others requiring twenty-four-hour care and possible use of restraint, seclusion, and/or isolation, such as

Recent suicide attempt and/or serious gesture with specific plan and means indicating current suicidal risk; or

Homicidal and/or dangerously assaultive behavior with specific threat and/or plan and available means indicating current homicidal risk; or

Life-endangering self-mutilative, self-destructive, or impulsive behavior; or

Current suicidal ideation and plan with a history of previous suicide attempts, serious gestures, and/or familial history of suicide; or

Current homicidal ideation and plan with history of dangerously assaultive behaviors

and

Client is unable to exhibit adequate age-appropriate behavioral control; and

Client is unable to maintain safety of self or others

and if

Client's support network is assessed to be inadequate to ensure client's safety and meet client's needs while away from a structured therapeutic program; and/or

Professional psychotherapeutic resources are not otherwise available or sufficient to ensure client's safety and meet client's needs while away from a structured program; and

Anti-social diagnoses and referrals to police or juvenile authorities have been ruled out

Level of care recommended: Acute inpatient

Note: Lack of placement, in and of itself, is never sufficient reason to hospitalize.

Goals of admission:

Stabilization and transfer to a less restrictive level of care via initiation or maintenance on psychopharmacological regimes, psychotherapeutic interventions utilizing individual, group, and family modalities as needed, and other adjunctive acute therapies, which may include occupational therapy, art therapy, and so on
Continued evaluation of support network with mobilization of resources to strengthen existing support network to prepare for client's reentry into the community
Immediate and thorough family assessment with treatment as indicated
Immediate and aggressive discharge planning

Degree of Impairment: Moderate to Moderately Severe
Moderate to moderately severe disturbance in one or more of the following: affect, behavior, thought processes, and judgment, such that

Client's basic survival needs cannot be provided independent of a twenty-four-hour structured therapeutic program; and
Client is experiencing significant interference in familial, educational, and other age-appropriate functions due to the severity of the symptoms; and
Client's history and developmental abilities indicate that he or she is capable of greater age-appropriate functioning and is assessed to be likely to show improvement with therapeutic interventions;

nonetheless

Client is able to participate in treatment planning and is compliant with treatment recommendations in an age-appropriate manner; and
Client's family or guardian is able to participate in the treatment process.

and/or

Moderate risk of suicide and/or harm to others requiring twenty-four-hour observation and support, such as

Current suicidal ideation without plan; may include a history of gestures or attempts; or

Current homicidal ideation without specific plan and/or assaultive behavior or impulses that the client is unable to contain independent of twenty-four-hour support and structure; or

Recurrent episodes of self-mutilative behavior in which the frequency and severity of the behavior warrant twenty-four-hour observation and care; or

Impulsive behavior that is potentially self-endangering that is not age-appropriate and is the result of a psychiatric diagnosis

and

Client is unable to exhibit adequate age-appropriate behavioral control without assistance of a structured twenty-four-hour program; and

Client is unable to maintain safety of self or others without twenty-four-hour therapeutic structure and support

and if

Support network that is not adequate to ensure client's safety and meet client's needs while client is away from a structured therapeutic program, yet client is willing to actively participate as directed and comply with treatment recommendations; and/or

Professional psychotherapeutic resources are not otherwise available or sufficient to ensure client's safety and meet client's needs while away from a structured program; and

Anti-social diagnoses and referrals to police or juvenile authorities have been ruled out or are in the process of being evaluated.

Level of care recommended: Residential

Note: Lack of placement, in and of itself, is never sufficient reason for placement in a residential treatment program.

Goals of admission:

Stabilization, reduction in severity of symptoms, improvement in levels of age-appropriate functioning, and transfer to a less restrictive level of care, via maintenance on psychopharmacological regimes, psychotherapeutic interventions utilizing individual, group, and family modalities as needed, and other adjunctive therapies, which may include occupational therapy, art therapy, and so on

Continued evaluation of support network with mobilization of additional resources to strengthen existing support network to facilitate client's reentry into the community

Immediate and thorough family assessment with treatment as indicated
Immediate and thorough discharge planning.

Degree of Impairment: Moderate

Moderate disturbance in one or more of the following: affect, behavior, thought processes, and judgment, such that

> Client's needs can be met outside of a structured therapeutic program for limited periods only and require the intervention and management of a structured program beyond one hour a day; and
> Client is experiencing interference in familial, educational, and other age-appropriate functions due to the severity of the symptoms; and
> Client's history and developmental abilities indicate that he or she is capable of greater age-appropriate functioning and is assessed to be likely to show improvement with therapeutic interventions;

> nonetheless

> Client is able to participate in treatment planning, comply with treatment recommendations, and utilize the treatment process in an age-appropriate manner; and
> Client's family or guardian is able to participate in the treatment process

and/or

Moderate risk of suicide and/or harm to others requiring therapeutic intervention and observation beyond one hour per day, such as

> Current suicidal ideation without a specific plan, may include a history of suicidal gestures; or
> Current homicidal ideation without a specific plan and/or assaultive impulses that the client is able to contain only with daily structured support and therapeutic intervention; or
> Impulsive behavior that is potentially self-endangering that is not age appropriate
> Recurrent self-mutilative behavior that is potentially self-endangering that can only be safely contained with structured, intensive therapeutic intervention; or
> Impulsive behavior that is potentially self-endangering that is not age appropriate and is a result of a psychiatric disorder;

and

> Client is able to exhibit limited age-appropriate behavioral control only with structured, intensive therapeutic intervention; and

Client's ability to contract for safety of self or others while away from a structured therapeutic program is adequate.

and if

Support network is available to provide only limited care, support, and supervision to ensure client's safety while away from a structured therapeutic program; and/or
Support network is willing to actively participate in client's therapy, comply with treatment recommendations, and not interfere with the treatment process.

Level of care recommended: Partial hospitalization or day treatment

Goals of admission:

Stabilization, reduction in severity of symptoms, improvement in levels of age-appropriate functioning, and transfer to outpatient care, via maintenance on psychopharmacological regimes, psychotherapeutic interventions utilizing individual, group, and family modalities as needed, and other adjunctive therapies, which may include occupational therapy, art therapy, and so on
Continued evaluation of support network with mobilization of additional resources to strengthen existing support network to facilitate client's independent functioning within the community
Immediate and thorough family assessment with treatment as indicated
Ongoing discharge planning.

Degree of impairment: Mild to moderate
Mild to moderate disturbance in one or more of the following: affect, behavior, thought processes, and judgment, such that

Client's needs can be adequately provided for outside of a structured therapeutic program; and
Client is experiencing some impairment in familial, educational, and other age-appropriate levels of functioning due to the symptoms of a psychiatric disorder; or
Client is functioning adequately in all spheres but expresses significant subjective distress such that therapeutic intervention is warranted

nonetheless

Client is able to participate in the treatment planning and process in an age-appropriate manner; and
Client's family or guardian is able to participate in the treatment process

and/or

Mild to moderate risk of suicide and/or harm to others requiring therapeutic intervention, such as

Suicidal ideation without specific plan or means; or
Assaultive impulses or behavior without specific threat and/or plan; or
Impulsive or self-destructive behavior that does not seriously endanger the client

and

Client exhibits adequate age-appropriate behavioral control; and
Client is able to contract for safety of self and others in an age-appropriate manner

and if

Support network is adequate to ensure client's safety and meet client's needs; and/or
Support network is willing to actively participate in the client's therapy, comply with treatment recommendations, and not interfere with the treatment process.

Level of care recommended: Outpatient

Goals of admission:

Stabilization, reduction in severity of symptoms, and improvement such that client functions age-appropriately in all spheres independent of any regular psychiatric interventions, via maintenance on psychopharmacological regimes, psychotherapeutic interventions utilizing individual, group, and family modalities as needed
Continued evaluation of support network with mobilization of additional resources to strengthen existing support network to facilitate client's age-appropriate functioning within the community
Ongoing family assessment with treatment as indicated
Increased utilization of client's support network and community resources.

LEON WANERMAN, M.D., is deputy medical director at U.S. Behavioral Health and clinical professor of psychiatry at the University of California, San Francisco.

Evidence is increasing that managed mental health care is cost-effective for direct mental health expenditures and for decreasing medical costs, especially for persons with chronic medical conditions.

Managed Mental Health, Medicaid, and Medical Cost Offset

Michael S. Pallak, Nicholas A. Cummings, Herbert Dörken, Curtis J. Henke

An extensive literature (Jones and Vischi, 1979; Mumford and others, 1984) suggests that mental health treatment may reduce the utilization and cost of medical services. The classic Kaiser Permanente studies (Follette and Cummings, 1967; Cummings and Follette, 1968; Cummings and Follette, 1976) demonstrated that patients who initiated mental health treatment had higher medical cost and service utilization histories prior to treatment. Compared to matched controls, the medical costs of patients with one to eight managed mental health treatment visits declined in the following year and remained at these lower levels for five years. The effect has been obtained in a growing number of studies (Mumford and others, 1984; Holder and Blose, 1987).

In general, the simple explanation for the cost-offset effect (so named because, at some point, the reduction in medical costs may offset the cost of providing mental health services) hinges on the view that patients under emotional distress seek relief through the use of medical services. In this view, patients may present with physical symptoms in an attempt to find relief from emotional distress or may just be looking for a "port in a storm."

This research was supported by the Health Care Financing Administration (HCFA) Contract No. 11-C-98344/9 to the State of Hawaii, for which the Foundation for Behavior Health was the subcontractor. While the final report has been accepted by the State of Hawaii and by the HCFA, the present results and conclusions do not necessarily reflect the opinions of either agency. Preparation of the analyses and contract report was the sole responsibility of the Foundation for Behavioral Health.

Their medical symptoms persist despite efforts to treat them, since the underlying and unrecognized emotional problems remain untreated. Mental health services may thwart this process by shifting the patient into treatment directly appropriate to the emotional problems, and medical costs decline as a result. To the extent that medical costs reflect untreated or inappropriately treated emotional distress, mental health treatment should reduce medical services utilization and costs. In this sense, reduction in medical services utilization reflects the efficacy of mental health treatment and provides an empirical measure of clinical outcome (Pallak and Cummings, in press).

The implications of the relationship between mental health services and medical costs also extend beyond triage of the patient into more appropriate treatment. Emotional distress may exacerbate symptoms of diagnosed biological or physical illness, while medical illness per se may trigger emotional distress that complicates the medical condition. Mental health services directed to these patients may also result in medical cost reduction.

For example, Schlesinger and others (1983) found that outpatient mental health services reduced medical costs for patients with confirmed chronic medical diagnoses of ischemic heart disease, hypertension, airway or respiratory problems, or diabetes. The decline in medical services costs was apparent within six months after the year in which the mental health services were initiated and continued for three years.

In general, these results suggest that effective programs could be implemented to reach out to higher-medical-utilizing subpopulations in order to encourage entry into mental health services. The issue from a policy perspective becomes the extent to which such programs may result in medical cost reduction relative to the cost of the outreach and mental health treatment.

The marginal utility of increased (rather than decreased) access to mental health services within an overall approach to health care has substantial implications for health policy in this country. For example, about 40 percent of the adult population may have one or more of the four chronic medical diagnoses investigated by Schlesinger and others (1983). As a result, the potential impact of mental health services may extend beyond the typical 2 to 4 percent penetration rates for outpatient mental health services to a substantially larger proportion of the population using medical services.

Almost without exception, studies of the relationship between mental health and the cost of medical services have been done with employed populations with some form of health insurance, either in HMO or fee-for-service settings (Mumford and others, 1984). In contrast, the research presented here was carried out with a Medicaid population, higher medical utilizers than the employed comparison population. For example, in the present study, Medicaid recipients had average annual medical costs that were about twice as high as an employed comparison population, which was about ten years older on the average (Cummings, Pallak, Dörken, and Henke, 1991).

In this study, managed mental health services were provided in an HMO (staff model) service setting using a brief-therapy adult developmental model. Although this approach is described more fully elsewhere (Cummings, 1991a, 1991b), an overview is presented here. As with managed mental health in general, this model matches the patient to an appropriate level of treatment intensity rather than automatically admitting to inpatient treatment. Outpatient treatment is preferable, since the patient and family are spared the dislocation, regression, and stigma associated with hospitalization (Pallak and Cummings, 1992). In brief therapy and in this model in particular, treatment consists of intermittent episodes, as needed, that meet crises occurring through the life cycle. The patient stops treatment when abilities to cope and function are restored. Therapeutic intervention during these crises is focused on helping the individual to develop more adequate methods of dealing with threats and transitions. As a result, the traditional concepts of "cure" and "termination" are not the goals of treatment. Rather, cessation of therapy is viewed as a planned interruption (because the emotional crisis has abated) rather than a termination.

Patients receive longer episodes of treatment, including inpatient treatment, *when needed.* Based on an on-site mental status exam, patients may be admitted to inpatient or referred to intensive outpatient treatment, often beginning immediately in the emergency room (Pallak and Cummings, 1992). Some sixty specific treatment protocols have been developed that are targeted to specific patient problems (Cummings, 1991b). Contrary to concerns that managed mental health may limit access to clinically necessary services, in this model it seeks to increase access to appropriate treatment before the patient deteriorates and requires more expensive and intensive treatment.

Mounting the Project

The State of Hawaii was an ideal site for the managed mental health/Medicaid research project for several reasons: (1) The Medicaid outpatient mental health benefit was generous—an annual benefit of twenty-four visits, with an additional twenty-four allowed on reauthorization. (2) The Medicaid research population could be delimited geographically on the island of Oahu along with an employed comparison population. Enrollees had access to excellent public transportation. (3) The state had contracted with the same fiscal intermediary (the Hawaii Medical Service Association, HMSA) that had covered about half the Medicaid population from the beginning of the Medicaid plan, thereby ensuring continuity in the claims data base. (4) The Hawaii Medicaid plan had been stable with regard to benefits and recognized mental health providers—that is, psychiatrists, psychologists under physician prescription, and certain clinics. (5) The longitudinal claims data base available through HMSA was comprehensive and detailed for both medical and mental health services. Each instance of payment for physician office visits, mental health outpatient visits, emergency room visits, diagnostic procedures, hospital days, controlled drug prescriptions, and medical costs could be extracted. (6) Between 1980 and 1983, Hawaii Medicaid costs had increased by 57 percent. Medical expenditures were $171.6 million in 1984, and in 1983 Medicaid expenditures represented 43 percent of welfare expenditures on Oahu. For fiscal year 1984–85, the state reported "psychiatric" Medicaid expenditures of $11.47 million, with $7.76 million of that for hospital inpatient or nursing home services. About 8 to 12 percent of the Medicaid population had used, or were using, mental health services (Cummings, Pallak, Dörken, and Henke, 1991).

Project Design

The experimental design was prospective and randomized. About two-thirds of the Medicaid population available through HMSA were randomly assigned (by family) to the experimental group. The experimental intervention consisted of full coverage under Medicaid for managed mental health services directly available without physician referral, copayment, deductible, or maximum-limit requirements. Access to managed mental health services did not restrict access to unmanaged mental health services by other providers under Medicaid.

Although a prospective design, two elements made the project quasi-experimental. First, while two-thirds of the Medicaid population were randomly assigned to eligibility for the additional managed benefit, patients still "self-selected" into usage of the benefit. A true experimental design would have randomly assigned patients who had already decided to use mental health services to one of the treatment alternatives (managed or unmanaged) or to no mental health treatment, despite the obvious ethical problems with the latter.

The second element involved outreach as a case acquisition method. From a policy perspective, one goal of the project was to assess likely outcomes if managed mental health services were available on a programmatic basis within Medicaid. The "bottom-line" policy perspective incorporated in the project necessitated outreach efforts directed at high medical utilizers— for example, those with one or more of the four chronic medical diagnoses studied by Schlesinger and others (1983). As a result, Medicaid enrollees who used project-managed mental health services would be expected to have histories of greater medical cost than enrollees who never used mental health services or than enrollees who used unmanaged services.

Within this framework, we compared patterns of medical cost for Medicaid enrollees randomly assigned to the experimental condition who used managed mental health services with enrollees in the control condition who never used treatment and those who used unmanaged mental health services. Since Medicaid recipients were not restricted in utilization, we also identified a subset of enrollees who used services from both managed and unmanaged providers at some point. While the exact type of unmanaged provider was not extracted for enrollees using such services, approximately 67 percent of all Medicaid outpatient visits were provided by psychiatrists in 1983 (Dörken and Cummings, 1986), the year prior to the initiation of the project.

Medical cost and utilization data were aggregated by six-month calendar periods, by individual. The calendar period in which treatment was initiated was designated as the managed mental health period. A change score was derived by subtracting cost or utilization in the twelve-month pre–managed mental health period from the twelve-month post–managed care period. Since treatment may have been initiated early or late in the managed care period (the exact calendar date of the first unmanaged care visit was not extracted from the claims file), the relationship between managed mental health care and medical cost/utilization was ambiguous in this period and these data were set aside.

Data from Medicaid recipients who never used treatment were aggregated in a similar fashion. The results discussed below for medical costs are presented in 1983 constant dollars to have a more precise picture of trends, undistorted by inflation or other secular influences on medical costs.

Clinical Staff. Staff who provided the managed mental health services were recruited locally and, because of the relatively short duration of the project, retained ties to their own practice on a half-time basis. A total of eight personnel (four FTEs) formed the project clinical staff. They received intensive training in managed mental health services prior to the initiation of the services. All clinical psychologists were licensed, had doctorates, and were Oahu residents. Two psychiatrists were consultants from the outset, and two additional psychiatrists were retained for direct clinical intervention with medical problems.

Clinical Diagnoses and Procedures. The project's clinical services began in April 1984 and continued to July 1987. While diagnostic information was not extracted from the claims file for patients who received unmanaged mental health services, diagnostic information was maintained for managed care patients.

In the first half-year of service, diagnoses of schizophrenia and affective psychoses accounted for 24.2 percent (21.4 percent and 2.8 percent, respectively) of patients seen. As might be expected based on prevalence rates, these patients were referred early in the project period in response to the notification of benefit. The percentage declined subsequently to about 8 percent (5.6 percent and 2.4 percent, respectively) in the second half of 1986 and to 4.5 percent (3.2 percent and 1.3 percent, respectively) in the first half of 1987, reflecting the fact that prevalence exceeded incidence (that is, the number of patients already diagnosed exceeded the number of new ones).

The percentage with a diagnosis of depression fluctuated between 16.3 percent in the second half of 1985 and a high of 20.9 percent in the first half of 1986. Over the course of the project, depression was the most frequent diagnosis and accounted for about 19 percent of all patients.

As indicated by encounter forms and patient charts, about 44 percent of all procedures were individual psychotherapy. With a developing caseload, group therapy reached a 20 percent level by the last half of 1985 and remained at that level. Medical treatment in the form of drugs accounted for 8 percent of all procedures and was primarily directed toward maintenance and stabilization of psychotic patients. Family therapy accounted for about 2 percent of all procedures, and psychological testing accounted for only 1 percent. Telephone consultations accounted for about 9 percent and biofeedback about 10 percent. Thus, the orientation to providing the treatment needed for the patient's specific problem accounted for the substantial differences in the types of treatment provided.

Results

A total of 1,444 Medicaid recipients received managed mental health services during the project. The frequency and percentage of Medicaid enrollment by mental health treatment status and by medical diagnosis, age, gender, and Medicaid eligibility category are summarized in Table 3.1.

Characteristics of Medicaid Recipients. As indicated in Table 3.1, the three primary groups in the study consisted of those who received no mental health services, those who received unmanaged services, and those who received managed services. There was also a small subgroup that received both managed and unmanaged services. Relative to those who received no services, those that received unmanaged services were more likely to be male ($p < .0001$), be eighteen to fifty-nine years old ($p < .0001$), receive assistance under the ABD and GA Medicaid categories ($p < .001$), and have a chronic medical disorder diagnosis ($p < .0001$).

Relative to the group that did not use mental health services, those who used either managed or both unmanaged and managed mental health services were more likely to be female ($p < .0001$), be eighteen to fifty-nine years old but even more likely to be over 60 ($p < .0001$), be AFDC recipients ($p < .001$), have a chronic medical disorder diagnosis ($p. < .001$).

Relationship Between Treatment Status and Length of Medicaid Enrollment. In general, those who used mental health services (managed or not) had longer periods of eligibility for Medicaid than enrollees who never used mental health services.

The mean length of Medicaid enrollment for the no-treatment group was 29.04 months. For the unmanaged-services group, it was 34.32 months.

The length of Medicaid enrollment for the managed-services group was 43.08 months, 148 percent of that for the no-treatment group ($p. < .0001$)

Table 3.1. Medicaid Enrollee Characteristics by Mental Health Treatment Status for All Enrollees Regardless of Length of Medicaid Enrollment

| | Type of Treatment | | | |
	No Treatment	Unmanaged	Managed	Managed and Unmanaged
N	26,258	3,614	749	680
%	100%	100%	100%	100%
Medical Diagnosis				
Chronic medical disease	7,089	1,368	404	369
	27.0%	37.9%	53.9%	54.1%
Nonchronic medical disease	18,965	1,479	327	196
	72.2%	40.9%	43.7%	28.8%
Chemical dependency	204	767	18	116
	0.8%	21.2%	2.4%	17.1%
Age				
0–17	15,220	719	158	32
	58.0%	19.9%	21.1%	4.7%
18–59	8,668	2,755	526	629
	33.0%	76.2%	70.2%	92.5%
60+	2,370	140	65	19
	9.0%	3.9%	8.7%	2.8%
Gender				
Female	15,220	1,893	539	424
	58.3%	52.4%	72.0%	62.4%
Male	10,959	1,721	210	256
	41.7%	47.6%	28.0%	37.6%
Eligibility Category[a]				
AFDC	18,180	1,297	457	195
	69.2%	35.9%	61.0%	28.7%
ABD	2,572	676	122	176
	9.8%	18.7%	16.3%	25.9%
GA	1,822	1,318	107	281
	6.9%	36.5%	14.3%	41.3%
Other	3,684	323	63	28
	14.0%	8.9%	8.4%	4.1%

Note: Stratifications by medical diagnosis, age, are not independent and sum to 100 percent in each.

[a]AFDC = Aid to Families with Dependent Children; ABD = Aged, Blind, or Disabled; GA = General Assistance.

and 126 percent of that for the unmanaged-services group ($p < .0001$). There was no reliable difference between the managed-services group and those who used both managed and unmanaged services.

Relationship Between Use of Mental Health Services and Medical Costs. These results represent the cost of medical services excluding the costs of mental health services rendered by either managed or unmanaged providers. Thus, medical cost comparisons are not confounded by mental health costs. The relationship between mental health treatment costs and medical costs is examined in a later section.

The project provided services to a total of 1,444 Medicaid recipients. Of these, 711 (49.24 percent) were continuously eligible for at least thirty months, and the remainder were eligible either intermittently or for shorter periods of time. Since 95 percent of the Medicaid mental health service users had a medical claim in the year preceding their mental health treatment, we did not disaggregate by this dimension.

The results for medical cost and changes in medical cost for the thirty-month Medicaid eligibility cohort are summarized in Table 3.2. Analyses were first carried out as a one-way analysis of variance, which in all cases indicated reliable differences among groups (and hence are not reported here).

Medical Costs Before Mental Health Treatment. Medicaid recipients who sought unmanaged mental health services had reliably greater medical costs in the year preceding their mental health treatment than the no-treatment group ($1,482 versus $848), consistent with the literature (Mumford and others, 1984).

As would be expected from the outreach efforts, the managed-services recipients had medical costs about 230 percent of those for the no-treatment group and about 132 percent of those for the unmanaged-services group.

Change in Medical Costs Relative to Mental Health Treatment. In the no-treatment baseline group, medical costs increased from $848 to $978

Table 3.2. Medical Services Costs for Medicaid Enrollees:
Before Mental Health Treatment, After Mental
Health Treatment, Change in Medical Services Costs,
and Percentage Change in Medical Costs, by Treatment Status

Group	N	Cost Before Treatment ($)	Cost After Treatment ($)	Change in cost ($)	Change in cost (%)
No treatment	11,236	$848	$978	+$129	+15.21%
Unmanaged treatment	410	1,482	1,434	−47	−3.17
Managed treatment	369	1,958	1,553	−406	−20.74
Managed and unmanaged treatment	342	2,774	2,510	−264	−10.79
SD		3,220		3,028	

Note: All costs are in 1983 constant dollars.

per year, an increase of 15.12 percent in 1983 constant dollars. There was no reliable difference between the managed-services group and those who received both managed and unmanaged services. Medical costs in these two groups, however, declined reliably in relation to the no-treatment group. Relative to the no-treatment baseline, the decline in medical costs for the managed-services group and those who received both managed and unmanaged mental health services represented a decline of 36 percent and 24.7 percent, respectively.

The decline for the unmanaged-services group was not reliably different from the decline for the no-treatment group.

Two points are worth noting about these results:

Attributing these results to regression artifacts (due to differential extremeness of the pre–mental health services cost levels) does not seem justifiable. There are several reasons for this. To begin with, these trends, based on two six-month data periods, held through longer comparison periods—for example, twenty-four months before and after mental health treatment. While it could be argued that extreme scores based on one data point might be expected to regress in a single subsequent six-month period, it is less likely that the artifact would hold for twelve- or twenty-four-month comparison periods (Cummings, Pallak, Dörken, and Henke, 1991).

In addition, not all reliably more extreme scores resulted in greater declines in medical costs; examples include the comparisons between the managed-services group and those that received both managed and unmanaged services, between the unmanaged-services and no-treatment groups, and between the chronic medical diagnosis (CMD) and non-CMD group. Finally, we found the same effects in an employed comparison population where pre–mental health treatment medical costs for patients who received managed versus unmanaged care did not differ.

Medical costs remained higher for patients who received mental health treatment than for those who did not. As in other investigations (Holder and Blose, 1987; Mumford and others, 1984), project patients, while declining substantially in medical costs following managed mental health treatment (relative to the pre–managed mental health cost levels), remained at higher cost levels than those who received no treatment. On the bases of mean costs per calendar period (a common actuarial or "bottom-line" accounting approach) rather than change in costs relative to initiation of mental health treatment (a more powerful procedure), it could be concluded (erroneously) that mental health treatment had little impact on medical costs. Similarly, in a regression analysis, initial pre–mental health treatment costs were the strongest predictor of post–mental health treatment medical costs, and accounted for the majority of variance, as might be expected.

Mental Health and Medical Costs Related to Chronic Medical Diagnoses. The results summarized in Table 3.3 disaggregate medical cost trends for Medicaid recipients with one or more of the four CMDs from those without these diagnoses (Non-CMDs).

Table 3.3. Medical Services Costs for Medicaid Enrollees
Disaggregated by Presence of Chronic Medical Diagnosis (CMD)
or Absence (Non-CMD), by Mental Health Treatment Status

Type of Mental Health Treatment	N	Cost Before Treatment ($)	Cost After Treatment ($)	Change in Cost ($)	Change in Cost (%)
CMD patients					
No treatment	4,307	$1,338	$1,694	+$356	+26.61%
Unmanaged	169	1,745	2,045	+300	+17.19
Managed	227	2,654	2,126	−528	−19.89
Managed and unmanaged	209	3,150	3,110	−40	−1.27
Non-CMD patients					
No treatment	6,837	533	511	−21	−3.94
Unmanaged	199	1,187	907	−280	−23.58
Managed	136	864	633	−231	−26.74
Managed and unmanaged	91	1,662	938	−724	−43.56
SD		3,220		3,028	

Note: Enrollees with a primary diagnosis of chemical dependency (CDP) are not included.

In the thirty-month eligibility cohort of 36,103, a total of 13,501 (37.4 percent) were in the CMD category. Among the unmanaged-services group, a total of 368, or 46 percent, were in the CMD category. Finally, of the managed-services patients, a total of 61.3 percent were in the CMD category, again reflecting the outreach effort toward high medical utilizers. Overall, mental health services users were more likely than non–mental health enrollees to have fallen in the CMD category.

As one would expect, Medicaid enrollees with chronic medical disease had higher medical costs than those without it. For example, within the no-treatment group, medical costs for those with CMDs were 251 percent of those without CMDs. Within the CMD category, medical costs for the unmanaged-services group and the no-treatment group did not differ reliably. Within the unmanaged-services group, medical costs for those with CMDs were greater than for those without CMDs.

Change in Medical Costs for the CMD Group. Within the CMD group, medical costs for the no-treatment group increased to 127 percent of those prior to the inception of the project. Medical costs for the unmanaged-services group increased to 117.2 percent of those pre–mental health treatment, and there was no reliable difference between the no-treatment and the unmanaged-services groups. In contrast, medical costs in the managed-services group and those in the subgroup that used both managed and unmanaged services declined relative to the no-treatment baseline and relative to the unmanaged-services group.

The decline obtained in those with CMDs who received managed mental health services and those with CMDs who received both managed and unmanaged services represented an absolute decline of 10.17 percent and a decline of 36.78 percent in medical costs relative to the no-treatment baseline of 26.61 percent.

Change in Medical Costs for the Non-CMD Group. Within the non-CMD group, medical costs declined by 3.94 percent for the no-treatment group and by 23.58 percent for the unmanaged-services group. While the difference between the two groups was not reliable (–280 versus –21, t = 1.19), the decline was about the same as that obtained for the managed-services group.

Medical costs in the managed- and unmanaged-services groups (pooled) declined relative to those for the no-treatment group. The declines were about 27 percent and 44 percent, or, relative to the no-treatment baseline, about 23 percent and 39 percent, respectively.

Relationship Between Mental Health Services Costs and Reduced Medical Costs. The simplest measure of the relationship between the costs of providing mental health services and a change in medical services costs is the average reimbursement for a mental health visit under Medicaid. In 1983 constant dollars, the State of Hawaii reimbursed $48 per such visit.

Managed mental health patients used 3.75 visits for a total cost of $180 (3.75 × $48). As indicated in Table 3.2, their medical costs declined by $406 relative to the pre–mental health treatment period. Thus, the cost of providing managed mental health services to this group was recovered in about 0.44 years, or 5.32 months, in absolute dollars.

However, for the no–mental health treatment baseline, medical costs increased by $129 per year. Relative to the no-treatment baseline, costs for the managed-services group were recovered in 0.34 years, or about 4 months.

The unmanaged-services patients used a total of 12.2 visits for a cost of $586.60. Their medical cost declined by $47. Thus the mental health service costs were recovered in about 12.5 years in absolute dollars and in about 3.33 years relative to the no-treatment baseline. The magnitude of these data projected forward, even with a modest inflation rate of 7 percent, would double these numbers.

It seems clear that managed mental health services resulted in recovery of their costs within reasonable time periods. While the length of the recovery period varied with the type of mental health services, the recovery period for managed mental health services was short relative to the total length of Medicaid enrollment.

Discussion

As indicated in this project, managed mental health services consistently resulted in declines in medical costs for Medicaid enrollees. These declines were associated with inpatient hospital days and outpatient services, including physician office visits. Controlled drug prescriptions and emergency room visits also declined (the data are not presented here) (Cummings, Pallak, Dörken, and Henke, 1991).

In contrast, traditional unmanaged mental health services had little effect on medical costs overall. In the more extensive analyses (Cummings, Pallak, Dörken, and Henke, 1991), we found that unmanaged mental health services resulted in reliable declines in inpatient hospital days equal to the decline obtained for managed care patients. However, for unmanaged care patients, these declines were also associated with reliable increases in outpatient services, including physician office visits, controlled drug prescriptions, and emergency room visits. We are continuing analyses for subsets with longer periods of eligibility to assess whether these increases attenuate at some point.

The disaggregation by CMDs versus non-CMDs partially offset case mix or medical severity and provided a more detailed picture of trends for medical costs for mental health patients. For both CMD patients and non-CMD patients, managed mental health services produced reliable reductions in medical costs. In contrast, for CMD patients who received unmanaged mental health services, medical costs increased by 17 percent. For non-CMD patients, however, unmanaged mental health services produced declines in medical costs of about 24 percent, about the same decline as for the managed mental health care group.

These results are important because 37 percent of the Medicaid population fell into the CMD group and so could benefit from managed mental health intervention. In addition, Medicaid recipients who used mental health services spent substantially longer periods of time on Medicaid and were generally higher medical utilizers than those who received unmanaged mental health services. It should be clear that the problems that lead Medicaid enrollees to mental health services are likely to ensure that they remain on Medicaid for long periods of time. Implementing managed mental health treatment for this subset of enrollees, coupled with outreach to increase access, seems an obvious strategy for managing medical costs in Medicaid.

Within the Medicaid population, managed mental health services patients consistently used fewer outpatient visits than unmanaged mental health services patients. For the subgroup of patients who used both managed and unmanaged mental health services, the number of unmanaged visits used was 10 percent less than for the group that used unmanaged mental health visits only, representing additional cost savings. Relative to costs in the mental health treatment baseline, the cost of managed mental health services was offset by reductions in medical costs within five months for the group that used managed mental health services only and within twelve months for the subgroup that used managed and unmanaged mental health services.

Although not a full report of the extensive project results (Cummings, Pallak, Dörken, and Henke, 1991), the data presented here highlight at least two major health policy alternatives. The first is that managed mental health treatment has substantial implications for managing medical as well as mental health care costs within Medicaid.

The second is that the implications of these results extend well beyond the typical mental health treatment–utilizing subpopulations, whether in the Medicaid or employed population. The substantial 37 to 40 percent of the population with one or more of the CMDs obviously can benefit from managed mental health treatment. It is equally clear, however, that traditional unmanaged mental health treatment (as in the unmanaged-services groups here) has little impact on medical costs for this substantial subpopulation, perhaps explaining the lack of effect obtained by Fiedler and Wight (1989).

Ideally, Medicaid systems could identify subsets of enrollees utilizing high amounts of medical care either by diagnosis (for example, CMDs) or by overall levels of medical utilization per year (for instance, the upper 15 to 20 percent). In turn, outreach efforts by mail—or, more feasibly, through case worker referral—would draw a predictable percentage of high utilizers into mental health services. In tandem, brief training for eligible mental health providers could be initiated and directed specifically to the emotional problems associated with CMDs, somatization (psychological problems manifesting physically), and so on. These efforts could be managed on a pilot basis to refine and adapt these steps within specific Medicaid programs with an eye toward balancing the costs of intervention with medical cost reductions. In addition, it would be advantageous to train primary care physicians so that they can better refer for mental health care.

These steps do not represent a panacea for medical cost trends within Medicaid. While managed mental health services produced substantial declines in medical costs, which continued for at least two years following the intervention (Cummings, Pallak, Dörken, and Henke, 1991), mental health treatment users remained at higher levels of medical utilization than the average in the no-treatment group. Obviously, these enrollees continued to need medical services to a greater extent than other subsets of the Medicaid population.

However, when all the medical cost increase in a Medicaid population can be attributed to an identifiable subset, such as enrollees with CMDs (recall that non-CMD enrollees showed a 4 percent decline in constant dollars), the policy and program implications become clear. Increased access to managed mental health treatment holds substantial promise for managing medical costs in both a clinical and a cost-effective fashion.

References

Cummings, N. A. "Arguments for the Financial Efficacy of Psychological Services in Health Care Settings." In R. G. Rozensky, J. J. Sweet, and S. M. Tovian, (eds.), *Handbook of Clinical Psychology in Medical Settings.* New York: Plenum, 1991a.

Cummings, N. A. "Brief, Intermittent Therapy Throughout the LIfe Cycle." In C. Austad, and W. H. Berman, (eds.), *Psychotherapy in HMOs: The Practice of Mental Health in Managed Care.* Washington, D.C.: American Psychological Association, 1991b.

Cummings, N. A., and Follette, W. T. "Psychiatric Services and Medical Utilization in a Prepaid Health Plan Setting: Part II." *Medical Care,* 1968, *6,* 31–41.

Cummings, N. A., and Follette, W. T. "Brief Psychotherapy and Medical Utilization." In H. Dörken and Associates, *The Professional Psychologist Today.* San Francisco: Jossey-Bass, 1976.

Cummings, N. A., Pallak, M. S., Dörken, H., and Henke, C. J. *The Impact of Psychological Services on Medical Utilization.* Health Care Financing Administration Contract No. 11-C-98344/9. Report. Baltimore: Health Care Financing Administration, 1991.

Dörken, H., and Cummings, N. A. "Impact of Medical Referral on Outpatient Psychological Services." *Professional Psychology: Research and Practice,* 1986, *17,* 431–435.

Fiedler, J. L., and Wight, R. B. *The Medical Offset Effect and Public Health Policy.* New York: Praeger, 1989.

Follette, W. T., and Cummings, N. A. "Psychiatric Services and Medical Utilization in a Prepaid Health Plan Setting." *Medical Care,* 1967, *5,* 25–35.

Holder, H. D., and Blose, J. O. "Mental Health Treatment and the Reduction of Health Care Costs: A Four-Year Study of U.S. Federal Employees' Enrollment with the Aetna Life Insurance Company." In R. M. Scheffler, and L. F. Rossiter, (eds.), *Advances in Health Economics and Health Services Research.* Vol. 8. Greenwich, Conn.: JAI Press, 1987.

Jones, K., and Vischi, T. "The Impact of Alcohol, Drug Abuse, and Mental Health Treatment on Medical Care Utilization: A Review of the Research Literature." *Medical Care,* 1979, *17* (12), supplement.

Mumford, E., Schlesinger, H., Glass, G., Patrick, C., and Cuerdon, T. "A New Look at Evidence About Reduced Cost of Medical Utilization Following Mental Health Treatment." *American Journal of Psychiatry,* 1984, *141,* 1145–1158.

Pallak, M. S., and Cummings, N. A. "Inpatient and Outpatient Psychiatric Treatment: The Effect of Matching Patients to Appropriate Level of Treatment on Psychiatric and Medical-Surgical Hospital Days." *Applied and Preventive Psychology,* 1992, *1,* 83–87.

Pallak, M. S., and Cummings, N. A. In S. A. Shueman, S. L. Mayhugh, and B. S. Gould (eds.), *Managed Behavioral Health Care: A Search for Precision,* in press.

Schlesinger, H., Mumford, E., Glass, G., Patrick, C., and Sharfstein, S. "Mental Health Treatment and Medical Care Utilization in a Fee-for-Service System: Outpatient Mental Health Treatment Following the Onset of a Chronic Disease." *American Journal of Public Health,* 1983, *73,* 422–429.

MICHAEL S. PALLAK, Ph.D., is dean of Graduate Student Affairs, California School of Professional Psychology; executive vice president, Foundation for Behavioral Health; and a partner in Quality Behavioral Health, Inc.

NICHOLAS A. CUMMINGS, Ph.D., is founding president, California School of Professional Psychology; president, Foundation for Behavioral Health; and founder of American Biodyne, Inc. He was principal investigator for the project presented here.

HERBERT DÖRKEN, Ph.D., formerly served as director of mental health in California and professor at Langley-Porter Institute. He was co–principal investigator for this project.

CURTIS J. HENKE, Ph.D., is a health economist and adjunct assistant professor in the Department of Medicine, University of California, San Francisco. He directed all data collection for this project.

This chapter details the efforts of Oregonians to demonstrate the rationality of including mental health coverage in a comprehensive health plan.

Managed Mental Health in the Oregon Health Plan

Bentson H. McFarland, Robert A. George, David A. Pollack, Richard H. Angell

The Oregon Health Plan has generated considerable interest in the public and professional media. When the federal government, on August 3, 1992, denied Oregon's initial request for a Medicaid waiver to implement the plan, editorials quickly appeared in the *New York Times,* the *Washington Post,* and the *Wall Street Journal.* One of the first questions for the presidential candidates in the 1992 television debates pertained to the Oregon Health Plan. Yet relatively little has been written about the mental health aspects of this new approach to setting priorities for health services (Lund, 1991; Moran, 1991a, 1991b; Pollack, 1991).

Work on the Oregon Health Plan began in 1987. The immediate stimulus was a tragedy involving a six-year-old boy who had leukemia and was felt to need a bone marrow transplant estimated to have a 10 percent probability of success. Although transplants were not ordinarily part of the Oregon Medicaid program at that time, a special appeal was made in 1988 to a committee of the legislature to provide funding. The legislature determined that the estimated $100,000 cost for this type of procedure would be better invested in prenatal care for 1,500 pregnant Medicaid clients (Callahan, 1990). The child died, but the 1989 session of the legislature was moved to begin a process for defining the basic health care that would be made available to all Oregonians.

The underlying motivation for the Oregon Health Plan is, of course, the crisis in the United States health care "system" (Aukerman, 1991; Broskowski, 1991; Families USA Foundation, 1991; Fuchs, 1992; Gleicher, 1991; Himmelstein and Woolhandler, 1989; Iglehart, 1992; Koop, Laszewski, and

Wennberg, 1992). As in the rest of the country, Oregon's health care system is expensive and inequitable. Out of a population of three million, 400,000 have no health insurance. Costs of care for the uninsured are shifted to employers and providers.

The heart of the Oregon Health Plan is a process for defining and redefining basic health care (Cotton, 1992; Hadorn, 1991; Nerenz and others, 1992). The plan is designed so that basic services are provided to all people below the federal poverty level who would be enrolled in an expanded Medicaid program. In addition, the enabling legislation requires all employers to offer "substantially similar" services to their employees beginning in 1995. The intent of the legislation is to provide a means for covering all Oregonians who are not currently enrolled in either private or public insurance programs. Specifically, the "working poor" are included in this plan.

The feature of the Oregon Health Plan that has stimulated considerable controversy is the prioritized list of services. The Oregon Health Services Commission is a body appointed by the governor with the charge of prioritizing health services. The commission chose to rank order diagnoses and their associated treatments based on considerations of effectiveness and cost. There has been considerable interest worldwide in this list, which has been praised (Callahan, 1990; George, 1991; Kitzhaber, 1991a, 1991b; Stason, 1991) and condemned (Daniels, 1991; Gibson, 1991; Schramm, 1992; Steinbrook and Lo, 1992) in numerous publications.

Financing the Oregon Health Plan is another area of considerable interest (U.S. General Accounting Office, 1992). The legislation states that the majority of Oregon Medicaid clients are expected to be enrolled in managed care entities funded through capitation. It is further presumed that the "working poor" who are to be covered in employer-based programs will also be enrolled in capitated payment plans. Employers will either "play" by purchasing their own coverage or "pay" by letting the state use a payroll tax to purchase insurance for employees. Insurance companies wishing to write health insurance in Oregon will be required to offer plans to the small employers that provide coverage "substantially similar" to that afforded Medicaid clients. It is estimated that at least 80 percent of those participating in the Oregon Health Plan will be enrolled in a capitated payment system of one sort or another (Office of Medical Assistance Programs, 1991).

As the system matures, the cost figures will come from providers' actual expenditures. Depending on the funding available, the legislature then draws a cutoff line. Treatment of conditions above the line are reimbursed under the Oregon Health Plan, while others will not be paid for by the state. The legislation includes modifications of the state's malpractice laws exempting providers from liability if they fail to provide services that are below the cutoff line. Estimates of the costs of each "condition-treatment pair" have been described by the consulting actuary (Hunt, 1991).

Health Service Priorities

Work on setting priorities for medical conditions and associated health services has been under way since 1989. This process has been described in several places (Cotton, 1992; Hadorn, 1991; Oregon Health Services Commission, 1991), so here we will provide only a summary. The initial objective was to obtain substantial public input into the process. Public opinion on the utility of medical treatments was to be linked with the data on costs and outcomes of optimal or no treatment. However, medical specialty groups (with the exception of psychiatry) declined to provide estimates of costs (and outcomes) of treatment that might be considered suboptimal. These non–mental health providers stated that they had no way of obtaining such data. In contrast, the mental health providers, led by the Oregon Psychiatric Association, did attempt to generate cost and outcome data for untreated (or suboptimally treated) mental disorders. While crude, the mental health data enabled the Health Services Commission to test the methodology and variations on it. The commission used three different approaches to setting priorities for mental disorders. These methods were based respectively on quality-of-life (that is, treatment-outcome) data only, quality of life divided by cost of optimal treatment, and net quality of life divided by net treatment costs. The last method attempted to account for the effects on quality of life and costs of not treating (or suboptimally treating) a condition (Kaplan and Anderson, 1988; LaPuma and Lawlor, 1990). Although the Health Services Commission was aware of the potential problems with its methodology, it proceeded to generate a list of physical health conditions based solely on quality-of-life and treatment-cost variables. As expected by the mental health community, the first list turned out to be seriously flawed. In response to substantial criticism (Daniels, 1991; Eddy, 1991; Fisher, Welch, and Wennberg, 1992; Steinbrook and Lo, 1992), the Health Services Commission then modified its methodology and produced its next document. This methodology is described elsewhere in some detail (Hadorn, 1991; Oregon Health Services Commission, 1991).

Revising the List

The Oregon Health Services Commission received notice on August 3, 1992, that the U.S. Department of Health and Human Services (DHHS) believed the process developed by the commission could violate the Americans with Disabilities Act (ADA), since quality-of-life judgments were used in formulating the list (Cotton, 1992; Hadorn, 1992). On questioning DHHS officials, it was learned that only the process was considered flawed, not the priority list itself. The list of condition-treatment categories is as follows:

1. Acute fatal; treatment prevents death, with full recovery
2. Maternity care
3. Acute fatal; treatment prevents death, without full recovery
4. Preventive care for children
5. Chronic fatal; treatment improves life span and quality of life
6. Reproductive services
7. Comfort care
8. Preventive dental care
9. Proven effective preventive care for adults
10. Acute nonfatal; treatment causes return to previous health state
11. Chronic nonfatal; one-time treatment improves quality of life
12. Acute nonfatal; treatment without return to previous health state
13. Chronic nonfatal; repetitive treatment improves quality of life
14. Acute nonfatal; treatment expedites recovery of self-limiting conditions
15. Infertility services
16. Less effective preventive care for adults
17. Fatal or nonfatal; treatment causes minimal or no improvement in quality of life

Although no discrimination had occurred in Oregon, the federal agency was fearful that the potential for bias might set an unacceptable precedent for other states that might, in the future, attempt to carry out a similar process. Although the Oregon Health Services Commission did not believe the original process had violated the ADA, the commission chose to revise its methodology to delete items of concern to DHHS so that the waiver process could proceed.

In keeping with DHHS requirements, the Health Services Commission removed from the data all of the original descriptors of symptoms and the public value weightings that had been obtained. Next, the commission set priorities for the condition-treatment pairs by the effectiveness of the specified treatment, measured solely by the change in health status due to the treatment. Effectiveness was rated on two criteria: (1) that the maintenance of life is of foremost importance, and (2) that if a condition exists, the most desirable state for a person with that condition is "asymptomatic" (as used in the data collection).

When ranking the condition-treatment pairs based on these criteria, the commission used only the following health outcomes data (reflecting the condition both with and without treatment as supplied by the health professionals): (1) the probability of death, (2) the probability of an asymptomatic state with the condition being considered, and (3) in case of ties, the medical cost to treat the condition. Condition-treatment pairs were ordered first on the ability to prevent death. In the event of a tie, the pairs were ordered on the ability of the treatment to return the patient to an asymptomatic state of health (after saving the person's life). If condition-treatment pairs were still tied, they were ordered based on the probability of treatment moving the patient from a symptomatic to an asymptomatic state. In the event of ties in all three effectiveness measures, the tied condition-treatment pairs were ordered on the average (medical) cost of the treatment, with the higher-cost pair being ranked lower.

The commissioners then reviewed these rankings on a line-by-line basis. Outside medical expertise was obtained for placement of some line items. In this review, the first consideration was that treatments preventing a condition, reducing additional complications or deterioration, or minimizing future costs should be ranked above other treatments for the condition. A second consideration was apparent incongruence of condition-treatment pairs with adjacent pairs. A third consideration was to rank the condition-treatment pairs where death was not a prominent issue according to agreed-on principles assimilated from the public input process. These principles included the following: (1) Maternal and child health were important public goals, and therefore related services were ranked in lines 50–74. (2) General preventive services for children and adults were ranked in lines 125–174. (3) Comfort care was considered important by Oregonians and was placed in lines 150–174. (4) Family planning was placed in lines 250–274. (5) The course of self-limited conditions does not usually change as a result of treatment, and these were therefore ranked in lines 600–624. (6) An additional consideration was medical significance of conditions that are contagious diseases or other public health risks. Condition-treatment pairs of this type were moved based on the collective judgment of the commission. For example, syphilis and tuberculosis were placed in lines 25–49. (7) The effectiveness of symptomatic relief in removing otherwise serious short-term symptoms of certain self-limited conditions such as labrynthitis was thought to justify a higher ranking for those condition-treatment pairs.

The new list was also submitted to the actuaries for repricing based on the revised rankings. The actuarial estimates and the final rankings were then presented to the Oregon legislature for reapproval and funding. Originally the legislature had authorized $130.46 per enrollee per month to support the Oregon Health Plan. This level of funding would have financed services through line 543. The legislature decided in early December 1992 to increase Medicaid funding by an additional $1.83 per beneficiary per month (for a total of $132.29). The additional funding moved the cutoff line to condition-treatment pair 568. This information was forwarded to DHHS on December 10, 1992.

The Medicaid waiver application was approved by the Clinton administration on March 19, 1993, with several provisos. One new federal requirement was that the state must provide a timetable for integrating mental health and chemical dependency services into the larger system. The Health Services Commission also made adjustments to the prioritized list, as requested by DHHS. Implementation of the Oregon Health Plan now awaits funding from the state legislature.

Mental Health and Chemical Dependency

The legislation establishing the Oregon Health Plan specified that mental health and chemical dependency conditions were not initially to be included. This position reflected several factors, including the preexistence of a public mental health system, concerns that mental health and chemical dependency services would be overused (Nerenz and others, 1992), a paradoxical belief that mental health and chemical dependency services were unneeded, and a concern that mental health and chemical dependency conditions could not be included in the priority-setting process. There was also uncertainty about the public's interest in treatment for these conditions. Thanks to a substantial lobbying effort by the Oregon Psychiatric Association, the final legislation included a provision that a subcommittee of the Health Services Commission would study the possible inclusion of mental health and chemical dependency services. This provision was a political trade-off. As a result, mandated mental health and chemical dependency treatments that must currently be included in conventional health insurance in Oregon will be discontinued when the integrated Oregon Health Plan (including mental health) is implemented.

An interesting early development was the clearly expressed desire on the part of the public for inclusion of mental health and chemical dependency. Telephone surveys showed that respondents ranked treatment of chemical dependency quite high and also favored inclusion of mental disorders in the top-priority items. Similar results were obtained from semistructured town hall meetings.

The Mental Health and Chemical Dependency Subcommittee of the Oregon Health Services Commission has operated in conjunction with and parallel to the overall process for the last three years. In addition, a coalition representing consumers, family members, major mental health and chemical dependency provider organizations, and the Oregon Mental Health Association has provided input to the Subcommittee's work.

Simultaneous with the gathering of input from the public, the mental health and chemical dependency providers began generating data on the costs and outcomes to be expected from treatment of mental health and chemical dependency disorders. Once again, the results were surprising to the Health Services Commission as a whole. As noted, the cost and outcome data for mental health and chemical dependency conditions appeared to be as (if not more) reliable and valid as the information about physical health conditions. When the initial, overly simplistic prioritization process failed to yield usable results for physical health problems as well as for mental health and chemical dependency, the Mental Health and Chemical Dependency Subcommittee began work on the rank ordering of mental health and chemical dependency conditions based on public opinion and clinical considerations (Lund, 1991; Mechcatie, 1992; Moran, 1991a, 1991b). This process resulted in the list shown in Exhibit 4.1. Furthermore, the subcommittee worked closely with the Health Services Commission to integrate this list into the complete prioritization of the condition-treatment pairs. .

The number preceding the name of each condition in Exhibit 4.1 indicates where the mental health or chemical dependency condition falls in the overall prioritized list that includes some 746 condition-treatment pairs. A comparison between the number of items shown in Exhibit 4.1 and the length of DSM-III-R indicates that there has been considerable lumping of mental health or chemical dependency disorders into the given line items. This same lumping process also occurred with the physical conditions. In contrast to the physical health conditions, there was no attempt to stratify by type of mental health or chemical dependency treatment—for example, psychotherapy versus pharmacotherapy. Conversely, for some physical health conditions, there may be cases where one type of treatment (for instance, surgery) was ranked lower than a different type of treatment (for example, medication) for the same condition. It should also be noted that some mental health conditions—such as major depression and conduct disorder—are represented more than once in the list, with more severe forms of the disorder (that is, those less amenable to treatment) generally receiving a lower ranking.

To aid in cost estimates, the mental health provider coalition—working in conjunction with the state mental health agency—developed a set of resource allocation guidelines for each of the mental disorders included in the list. A group of chemical dependency providers developed similar treatment guidelines for alcohol and drug abuse. The state mental health agency also conducted a survey of community mental health programs in order to provide their input into the process.

The guidelines (available from the authors) attempt to specify for each condition the number of hours of individual or family treatment or both to be provided to a typical consumer during the course of a year. Also, the guidelines estimate the fraction of consumers who will need additional services, such as local acute hospitalization, hospitalization in the state mental hospital, residential treatment, case management, skills training, and so on. The guidelines state that group treatment can be substituted for individual treatment, with one hour of group treatment being equivalent to twenty minutes of individual treatment.

The guidelines specify that all beneficiaries in the Oregon Health Plan are entitled to two hours of mental health and/or chemical dependency evaluation for adults and three hours for children. Further, the guidelines state that services for children (persons under age eighteen) should be provided only by individuals with special training.

Another of several parallel processes under way with regard to the Oregon Health Plan is the estimation of *treated* prevalence during a year for each of the mental health and chemical dependency conditions. The state mental health agency has compiled a spreadsheet showing expected numbers

Exhibit 4.1. Mental Health and Chemical Dependency Conditions in the Oregon Health Plan

The figure preceding the name of each condition refers to the condition's ranking in the prioritized list, while the figures following the name of each condition are the DSM-III-R code numbers.

115. Rumination disorder of infancy: 307.53
141. Abuse of or dependence on psychoactive substance: 303.90, 304.00, 304.10, 304.20, 304.30, 304.40, 304.50, 304.60, 304.90, 305.00, 305.20, 305.30, 305.40, 305.50, 305.60, 305.70
142. Major depression; single episode or mild: 296.20–296.26, 296.31, 311.00
143. Brief reactive psychosis: 297.30, 298.80, 298.90
144. Reactive attachment disorder of infancy or early childhood: 313.89
175. Schizophrenic disorders: 295.10–295.95
176. Major depression, recurrent: 296.30, 296.32–296.36
177. Bipolar disorders: 296.40–296.46, 296.50–296.56, 296.60–296.64, 296.66, 296.70
178. Attention deficit disorder with hyperactivity or undifferentiated: 314.00, 314.01
199. Anorexia nervosa: 307.10
200. Acute post-traumatic stress disorder: 309.89
201. Acute delusional mood anxiety, personality, perception and organic mental disorder caused by drugs; intoxication: 291.40, 292.11, 292.12, 292.89, 292.90, 303.00, 305.40, 305.50, 305.60, 305.70, 305.90
223. Chronic post-traumatic stress disorder: 309.89
297. Overanxious disorder: 313.00
321. Oppositional defiant disorder: 313.81
347. Conduct disorder, mild/moderate: solitary aggressive, group type, undifferentiated: 312.00, 312.20, 312.90
366. Eating disorder not otherwise specified: 307.50
367. Dissociative disorders: depersonalization disorder; multiple personality disorder; dissociative disorder not otherwise specified; psychogenic amnesia; psychogenic fugue: 300.12, 300.13, 300.14, 300.15, 300.60
368. Bulimia nervosa: 307.51
369. Panic disorder with and without agoraphobia: 300.01, 300.21
370. Anxiety disorder, unspecified; generalized anxiety disorder: 300.00, 300.02
371. Agoraphobia without history of panic disorder: 300.22
372. Tourette's disorder and tic disorders: 307.00, 307.20–307.23
373. Avoidant disorder of childhood or adolescence; elective mutism: 313.21, 313.23
374. Separation anxiety disorder: 309.21
375. Obsessive-compulsive disorder: 300.30
376. Conversion disorder, child: 300.11
377. Functional encopresis: 307.70
403. Paranoid (delusional) disorder: 297.10
404. Identity disorder: 313.82
421. Psychological factors affecting physical condition (for example, asthma, chronic GI conditions, hypertension): 316.00
422. Dysthymia: 300.40
423. Adjustment disorders: 309.00, 309.23, 309.24, 309.28, 309.30, 309.40, 309.82, 309.83, 309.90
424. Borderline personality disorder: 301.83
425. Chronic organic mental disorders: 292.11–292.12, 292.82–292.84, 292.89–292.90, 293.81–293.83, 310.10

Exhibit 4.1. (continued)

426. Simple phobia: 300.29
427. Social phobia: 300.23
428. Schizotypal personality disorders: 301.22
510. Stereotypy/habit disorder: 307.30
532. Somatization disorder; somatoform pain disorder: 307.80, 300.81
533. Sexual dysfunction: 302.70–302.76, 302.79
557. Impulse disorders: 312.31–312.34
632. Personality disorders excluding borderline, schizotypal, and anti-social: 301.00, 301.20, 301.40, 301.50, 301.60, 301.84, 301.90, 307.81–307.82
633. Gender identification disorder: 302.60, 302.85
660. Conduct disorder, severe: 312.00, 312.20, 312.90
661. Factitious disorders: 300.16, 300.19, 301.51
662. Hypochondriasis; somatoform disorder; not otherwise specified and undifferentiated: 300.70
663. Conversion disorder, adult: 300.11
719. Anti-social personality disorder: 301.70

Source: From the Oregon Health Services Commission's integrated, prioritized list of November 18, 1992.

of individuals (broken down by age and gender groups) who would typically receive treatment for a given condition during the course of a year. These data are taken from several epidemiologic studies, including the Epidemiologic Catchment Area Study (Robins and Regier, 1991) and the Ontario Health Study (Boyle and others, 1987; Offord and others, 1987; Szatmari, Offord, and Boyle, 1989), as well as from other work that has been published or is in progress (Bird and others, 1988; Costello, 1989; Institute of Medicine, 1989; Lewinsohn and others, 1992). It was surprising to discover how complete the period prevalence data were for mental health conditions. There are, however, significant gaps in the estimates of *treated* one-year-period prevalence. Where the data were unavailable, estimates were made. Also, descriptive prevalence rates from DSM-III-R were translated into approximate percentages, with "common" being equivalent to 1 percent, "uncommon" 0.1 percent, "rare" 0.01 percent, and "very rare" 0.001 percent. The treated prevalence estimates, in conjunction with the resource allocation guidelines and the price list, are used to produce an estimated cost for providing mental health and chemical dependency services to the enrolled population.

Implementation of this system is an ongoing challenge. As was mentioned, it is presumed that at least 80 percent of those covered by the Oregon Health Plan will be enrolled in capitated payment systems. The Oregon Psychiatric Association has proposed a model for such an integrated health and mental health system. It is hoped that this model will be specified in state regulations that define the nature of those health maintenance organizations eligible to participate in the Oregon Health Plan.

Essentially, the model states that beneficiaries are to be referred or can self-refer to a mental health–chemical dependency triage specialist. Such a person would typically have a master's degree and would be available twenty-four hours a day, seven days a week. The triage specialist would be supervised by a medical director with consultation from a multidisciplinary committee of mental health and chemical dependency providers. The triage specialist's main function is to determine whether hospitalization is indicated. If immediate hospitalization is required, the specialist authorizes three days of inpatient treatment, with any further hospital care subject to ongoing review by the multidisciplinary committee. Similarly, on outpatient care, the triage specialist would provide names of qualified providers capable of addressing the problem under the framework of the Oregon Health Plan. The initial evaluation (two hours for adults and three for children) includes a standardized data collection instrument and a request for further sessions (if needed) from the multidisciplinary committee. The committee would also be empowered to authorize additional services such as case management, residential treatment, group treatment, and so on. Ideally, the evaluator would also provide ongoing treatment unless patient needs dictated otherwise.

The managed care organization in which the beneficiary is enrolled under the Oregon Health Plan would be responsible for all aspects of physical and mental health care. However, the primary care provider is specifically not empowered to be a "gatekeeper" who might prevent enrollees from accessing mental health or chemical dependency services to which they are entitled. It is presumed that the managed care organization, or its subcontractors, will also be financially responsible for use of state mental hospital services.

The existence of a public mental health system operating parallel to the regular health care system is another challenge for the Oregon Health Plan. It is currently anticipated that some community mental health programs will become subcontractors to the larger managed care organizations in order to continue providing services, particularly to their "first-priority" population of chronically mentally ill individuals. The details of the subcontracting arrangements remain to be determined, particularly for those community mental health programs that function as branches of county government. Providers such as the managed care entity and presumably the first subcontractor level will be financially at risk under the capitated payment system. The state does intend to establish "stop-loss" mechanisms so that providers would share financial risk with the state for "outlier" or "high-user" clients.

Integration of Physical and Mental Health

Exhibit 4.2 provides examples of medical-surgical conditions that "bracket" the mental health items found in Exhibit 4.1. For instance, line 140 (pemphigus) precedes line 141 (abuse of or dependence on psychoactive substance). Hypertensive heart and renal disease (line 145) follows line 144 (reactive attachment disorder of infancy or early childhood). Heart failure (line 179) falls between attention deficit disorder with hyperactivity or undifferentiated (line

**Exhibit 4.2. Examples of Medical/Surgical
Condition-Treatment Pairs**

---

1. Severe/moderate head injury: hematoma/edema with loss of consciousness (medical and surgical treatment)
140. Pemphigus (medical treatment)
145. Hypertensive heart and renal disease (medical therapy)
174. End stage renal disease (medical therapy, including dialysis)
179. Heart failure (medical therapy)
198. Disorders of fluid, electrolyte, and acid-base balance (medical therapy)
224. Rupture of Achilles tendon or quadriceps tendon (repair)
296. Atrial septal defect, secundum (repair septal defect)
378. Rheumatoid arthritis, osteoarthritis, aseptic necrosis of bone (arthroplasty)
429. Giant cell arteritis, Kawasaki disease, hypersensitivity angitis (medical therapy)
509. Paralysis of vocal cords or larynx, other disease of larynx (incision, excision, endoscopy)
534. Osteoporosis (medical therapy)
568. Cancer of liver, treatable (medical and surgical treatment)
569. Lethal midline granuloma (medical therapy)
631. Mononeuropathy (medical therapy)
664. Redundant prepuce and phimosis (medical therapy, dilation)
716. Agenesis of lung (medical therapy)
720. Simple and unspecified goiter, nontoxic nodular goiter (medical therapy, thyroidectomy)
746. Sebaceous cyst (medical therapy)

---

178) and anorexia nervosa (line 199). Near the cutoff line are items 568 (cancer of liver, treatable) and 569 (lethal midline granuloma). These medical-surgical conditions lie between line 557 (impulse disorders) and line 632 (personality disorders excluding borderline, schizotypal, and anti-social).

The Oregon coalition of mental health and chemical dependency providers continues to work with the state mental health and Medicaid agencies in devising an appropriate delivery system. The system is expected to evolve over a number of years. Nonetheless, the goal of integration remains a high priority for consumers and family members as well as for mental health and chemical dependency professionals in both the public and the private sectors.

The Future

Stimulated by the legislation defining the Oregon Health Plan, at least one health maintenance organization has developed a "small employer protection plan" that includes some features "substantially similar" to those found in the proposed Medicaid program. For example, this package provides for mental health and chemical dependency coverage but states that "the number of visits depends on treatment protocols appropriate to the condition" (Kaiser Permanente, Northwest Region, 1992, p. 3).

Many aspects of the mental health and chemical dependency portion of the Oregon Health Plan are likely to be implemented in parallel with or even independently of the overall system. The state mental health agency has authority to implement payment for its Medicaid clients under a capitated system. Also, the current budgetary crisis at the state level provides a powerful incentive for changing the way public mental health services are financed. Under the present system, the state mental hospitals are supported almost entirely by state funds. Only the relatively few patients under age eighteen or over age sixty-five are covered by Medicaid or Medicare.

Under the Oregon Mental Health Plan, the state will shift to a capitated system. Each community mental health program will be assigned a list of clients for whom they are to be clinically and financially responsible. Reimbursement will be on a prospective basis. The community mental health programs will bear some degree of financial risk for use of the state hospital. It is clear that mental health and chemical dependency services in Oregon will change substantially over the new few years.

Addendum

After considerable acrimonious discussion, the legislature ended the longest session in Oregon's history by agreeing to fund the Medicaid portion of the plan. Sufficient state funds (augmented by a new tax on cigarettes) were appropriated to cover conditions through the equivalent of item number 660 (conduct disorder, severe) in Exhibit 4.1.

The physican health aspects of the Medicaid program will begin in February 1994. Chemical dependency services will become available in January 1995. As part of a phase-in program, mental health services will be made available to a quarter of the state's Medicaid clients starting in January 1995.

References

Aukerman, G. F. "Access to Health Care for the Uninsured: The Perspective of the American Academy of Family Physicians." *Journal of the American Medical Association,* 1991, *265,* 2856–2858.

Bird, H. R., Canino, G., Rubio-Stipec, M., Gould, M. S., Ribera, J., Sesman, M., Woodbury, M., Huertas-Goldman, S., Pagan, A., Sanchez-LaCay, A., and Moscoso, M. "Estimates of the Prevalence of Childhood Maladjustment in a Community Survey in Puerto Rico." *Archives of General Psychiatry,* 1988, *45,* 1120–1126.

Boyle, M. H., Offord, D. R., Hofmann, H. G., Catlin, G. P., Byles, J. A., Cadman, D. T., Crawford, J. W., Links, P. S., Rae-Grant, N. I., and Szatmari, P. "Ontario Child Health Study." *Archives of General Psychiatry,* 1987, *44,* 828–831.

Broskowski, A. "Current Mental Health Care Environments: Why Managed Care Is Necessary." *Professional Psychology: Research and Practice,* 1991, *22,* 1–9.

Callahan, D. *What Kind of Life: The Limits of Medical Progress.* New York: Simon & Schuster, 1990.

Costello, E. J. "Developments in Child Psychiatric Epidemiology." *Journal of the American Academy of Child and Adolescent Psychiatry,* 1989, *28,* 836–841.

Cotton, P. "'Basic Benefits' Have Many Variations, Tend to Become Political Issues." *Journal of the American Medical Association,* 1992, *268,* 2139–2141.

Daniels, N. "Is the Oregon Rationing Plan Fair?" *Journal of the American Medical Association,* 1991, *265,* 2332–2335.

Eddy, D. M. "Oregon's Methods: Did Cost-Effectiveness Analysis Fail?" *Journal of the American Medical Association,* 1991, *266,* 2135–2141.

Families USA Foundation. *Health Spending: The Growing Threat to the Family Budget.* Washington, D. C.: Families USA Foundation, 1991.

Fisher, E. S., Welch, H. G., and Wennberg, J. E. "Prioritizing Oregon's Hospital Resources: An Example Based on Variations in Discretionary Medical Utilization." *Journal of the American Medical Association,* 1992, *267,* 1925–1931.

Fuchs, V. "The Best Health Care System in the World?" *Journal of the American Medical Association,* 1992, *268,* 916–917.

George, R. A. "Health Care Rationing: Acceptable Option? 'Yes' " *Psychiatric News,* June 21, 1991, p. 14.

Gibson, R. W. "Health Care Rationing: Acceptable Option? 'No.' " *Psychiatric News,* June 21, 1991, pp. 14–15.

Gleicher, N. "Expansion of Health Care to the Uninsured and Underinsured Has to Be Cost-Neutral." *Journal of the American Medical Association,* 1991, *265,* 2388–2390.

Hadorn, D. C. "Setting Health Care Priorities in Oregon: Cost Effectiveness Meets the Rule of Rescue." *Journal of the American Medical Association,* 1991, *265,* 2218–2225.

Hadorn, D. C. "The Problem of Discrimination in Health Care Priority Setting." *Journal of the American Medical Association,* 1992, *268,* 1454–1459.

Himmelstein, D. U., and Woolhandler, S. "A National Health Program for the United States." *New England Journal of Medicine,* 1989, *320,* 102–108.

Hunt, S. "Pricing the Oregon Health Plan." *Contingencies,* Nov./Dec. 1991, pp. 37–45.

Iglehart, J. K. "Health Policy Report: The American Health Care System." *New England Journal of Medicine,* 1992, *326,* 962–967.

Institute of Medicine. *Research on Children and Adolescents with Mental, Behavioral, and Developmental Disorders: Mobilizing a National Initiative.* Washington, D.C.: National Academy Press, 1989.

Kaiser Permanente, Northwest Region. *Small Employer Protection Plan: Summary of Medical Benefits.* Portland, Oreg.: Kaiser Permanente, Northwest Region, 1992.

Kaplan, R. M., and Anderson, J. P. "A General Health Policy Model: Update and Applications." *Health Services Research,* 1988, *23,* 203–235.

Kitzhaber, J. A. "Constructive Debate in a Real World: Debate of New Health Policies Should Compare Each Proposal with Existing Systems as Well as with a Theoretical Ideal." *Health Management Quarterly First Quarter,* 1991a, *8,* 16–19.

Kitzhaber, J. A. "A Healthier Approach to Health Care." *Issues in Science and Technology,* 1991b, *7,* 59–65.

Koop, C. E., Laszewski, R. L., and Wennberg, J. E. "Health Care: Tinkering Won't Help." *Washington Post,* Feb. 19, 1992, p. A19.

LaPuma, J., and Lawlor, E. F. "Quality-Adjusted Life-Years: Ethical Implications for Physicians and Policymakers." *Journal of the American Medical Association,* 1990, *263,* 2917–2921.

Lewinsohn, P. M., Hops, H. H., Roberts, R. E., Seeleg, J. R., and Andrews, J. A. "Adolescent Depression I: Prevalence and Incidence of Depression and Other DSM-III-R Disorders in High School Students." Unpublished manuscript, Oregon Research Institute, Eugene, 1992.

Lund, D. "Oregon Legislature to Vote on Health Care Rationing List, Minus Mental Health Items." *Psychiatric Times,* May 1991, p. 86.

Mechcatie, E. "Oregon Plan Puts Care for Mental, Medical Ills on Equal Footing." *Clinical Psychiatry News,* Jan. 1992, pp. 15–16.

Moran, M. "MH Care Fares Well Under Revision of Oregon Plan." *Psychiatric News,* Apr. 19, 1991a, p. 1.

Moran, M. "Oregon Plan Forces Hard Choices, But Praised for Fairness, MH Coverage." *Psychiatric News,* May 3, 1991b, p. 15.

Nerenz, D. R., Zajac, B. M., Repasky, D. P., Williams, P. D., and Sahney, V. K. "Benefit Package Considerations in a State Health Care Plan." In J. H. Goodeeris and A. J. Hogan (eds.), *Improving Access to Health Care: What Can the States Do?* Kalamazoo: Mich.: Upjohn Institute, 1992.

Office of Medical Assistance Programs, Oregon Department of Human Resources. *Waiver Application: Oregon Medicaid Demonstration Project.* Salem: Office of Medical Assistance Programs, Oregon Department of Human Resources, 1991.

Offord, D. R., Boyle, M. H., Szatmari, P., Rae-Grant, N. I., Links, P. S., Cadman, D. T., Byles, J. A., Crawford, J. W., Blum, H. M., Byrne, C., Thomas, H., and Woodward, C. A. "Ontario Child Health Study. II: Six-Month Prevalence of Disorder and Rates of Service Utilization." *Archives of General Psychiatry,* 1987, *44,* 832–836.

Oregon Health Services Commission. *Prioritization of Health Services.* Salem: Oregon Health Services Commission, 1991.

Pollack, D. "Mental Health Services in the Oregon Plan: A Model for National Health Insurance." *Community Psychiatrist,* 1991, *5* (4), 4.

Robins, L. N., and Regier, D. A. *Psychiatric Disorders in America: The Epidemiologic Catchment Area Study.* New York: Free Press, 1991.

Schramm, C. J. "Oregon a Better Method to Reallocate Resources?" *Journal of the American Medical Association,* 1992, *267,* 1967.

Stason, W. B. "Oregon's Bold Medicaid Initiative." *Journal of the American Medical Association,* *265,* 1991, 2237–2238.

Steinbrook, R., and Lo, B. "The Oregon Medicaid Demonstration Project—Will It Provide Adequate Medical Care?" *New England Journal of Medicine,* 1992, *326,* 340–343.

Szatmari, P., Offord, D. R., and Boyle, M. H. "Ontario Child Health Study: Prevalence of Attention Deficit Disorder with Hyperactivity." *Journal of Child Psychiatry and Psychology,* 1989, *30,* 219–230.

U.S. General Accounting Office. *Medicaid: Oregon's Managed Care Program and Implications for Expansion.* Gaithersburg, Md.: U.S. General Accounting Office, 1992.

BENTSON H. MCFARLAND, M.D., Ph.D., *is associate professor of psychiatry, public health, and preventive medicine at Oregon Health Sciences University.*

ROBERT A. GEORGE, M.D., *is clinical associate professor of psychiatry at Oregon Health Sciences University, a member of the Oregon Health Services Commission, and a private practice child psychiatrist in Portland, Oregon.*

DAVID A. POLLACK, M.D., *is medical director of Mental Health Services West, Inc., adjunct professor of psychiatry at Oregon Health Sciences University, and a member of the Oregon Health Services Commission Mental Health and Chemical Dependency Subcommittee.*

RICHARD H. ANGELL, M.D., *is assistant professor of psychiatry and director of child psychiatry training at Oregon Health Sciences University.*

Employers have become the most enterprising of the payors for mental health care. A representative example is presented in this chapter.

Alcan Aluminum: Development of a Mental Health "Carve-Out"

Laura Altman, Wendy Price

During the past three years, the mental health "carve-out" (separating mental health from general medical benefits) has been a growing phenomenon. This strategy, initially adopted by Fortune 100 companies, is now being implemented by many others as well. A model mental health carve-out should have the following characteristics: a coordinated, managed approach to the provision of mental health and substance abuse (MHSA) care; a plan totally separate from the medical care plan; completely confidential assistance; a fully credentialed, carefully screened specialty network of high-quality MHSA practitioners and facilities; incentives to use the provider network through enhanced benefits that allow the maximum level of coverage; out-of-network benefits that provide a lower level of coverage; enhanced access to care—twenty-four hours a day, seven days a week—with a toll-free number staffed by MHSA clinicians who can either answer questions or refer the caller to a network practitioner; assistance at the time of the initial request in finding the most appropriate provider of MHSA care, based on matching the patient's needs with the provider's experience, expertise, and location; and little or no out-of-pocket cost and no claims form to file when a network provider is used.

Alcan Aluminum Corporation's experience in designing and implementing a managed mental health program illustrates how one company approached this managed care "voyage" by using a mental health carve-out as a first step toward managed care for all of its health benefits.

About the Company

Alcan Aluminum Corporation (Alcan), based in Cleveland, Ohio, is among the nation's leading integrated producers of primary and fabricated aluminum products. It is a wholly owned U.S. subsidiary of Alcan Aluminum Limited, Montreal, one of the world's largest aluminum companies.

Alcan offers its salaried employees a comprehensive benefit package, including health care and prescription drug benefits. The salaried health care plan covers 5,300 nonunion employees and early retirees. Benefits for union employees are covered by separate plans under collectively bargained agreements. Like most employers, over the years Alcan has implemented many initiatives, including self-funding, to control its health care costs.

By self-funding its medical program, Alcan has achieved greater control over its cash flow, paying claims as they are generated. Alcan's self-funded plan is considered an Employee Retirement Income Security Act (ERISA) plan and is preempted from state regulation. ERISA preemption confers the following advantages: exemption from state insurance premium taxes (otherwise levied on insured medical programs) and exemption from mandated health care coverages, which can include as many as fifty different benefits.

Benefit Objectives

Alcan's objectives for its U.S. salaried benefit program were developed when Alcan entered the U.S. market in the mid 1960s. They reflect Alcan's intent to maintain an organization of able and committed individuals while operating at a level of profitability that will ensure the company's long-term economic viability. Early in 1991, Alcan's board of directors gave its approval to an overall health care strategy based on the following benefit program objectives: be competitive with the benefit programs of other employers, meet the needs of the company's employees, and be within the company's ability to pay. Any proposed changes to existing benefit plans are measured against these three objectives.

Background to the Managed Care Decision

While influenced by its Canadian parent, Alcan's benefits philosophy was similar to that of many other companies in the United States during the 1980s. It was a traditional approach for both mental health and medical care, which is still in effect for medical benefits but was changed to the new MHSA managed care program at the beginning of 1993. The traditional mental health/substance abuse plan design is shown in Table 5.1.

In addition to these conventional benefits, which supported inpatient rather than outpatient treatment, several of Alcan's operating companies had employee assistance programs (EAPs). Whether and what kind of EAP to offer had always been the choice of each operating company; therefore, there were many different models and types within Alcan's operating companies.

In some work sites, drug testing programs had been introduced. Companywide, Alcan's policies included compliance with the Drug Free

**Table 5.1. Traditional Mental Health/Substance
Abuse Plan Design at Alcan**

	Traditional Coverage (Choice 1)	Comprehensive Coverage (Choice 2)
Mental Health/Substance Abuse		
Deductible	$100 single, $200 family; does not apply to all charges	$100 single, $200 family; applies to all charges
Out-of-pocket maximum	$500 per person for up to a two-year period; excludes deductible	$700 single, $1,400 family per calendar year; excludes deductible
Lifetime maximum	$1 million per covered member	$1 million per covered member
Mental Health		
Inpatient	100% reasonable and customary (R&C) for first $15,000, *then* 80% R&C to out-of-pocket maximum	80% R&C after deductible to out-of-pocket maximum
Outpatient	50% R&C after deductible; up to 52 visits per year; excluded from out-of-pocket maximum	50% R&C after deductible; up to 52 visits per year; excluded from out-of-pocket maximum
Substance Abuse		
Inpatient	100% R&C for first $15,000, then 80% R&C to out-of-pocket maximum; 45-day annual limit	80% R&C after deductible to out-of-pocket maximum; 45-day annual limit
Outpatient	50% R&C after deductible; up to a calendar year maximum of $1,000; excluded from out-of-pocket maximum	50% R&C after deductible; up to a calendar year maximum of $1,000; excluded from out-of-pocket maximum
	Additional treatment covered under outpatient MH provisions	Additional treatment covered under outpatient MH provisions

Workforce Act and Department of Transportation requirements where applicable.

A significant factor distinguished Alcan from many other companies. For several years, there had been an emphasis on collecting and analyzing health care data. Management was well aware, therefore, of its escalating health care costs and utilization trends, particularly in MHSA. As a result, at the outset of the strategic planning process, Alcan's senior management and benefits staff were in an excellent position to thoroughly analyze their experience, weigh multiple options, and make informed decisions.

The key findings derived from their data analyses had a major influence on the managed care decision. Table 5.2 displays the percent change in Alcan's medical and MHSA costs in a one-year period 1990–1991. An additional finding, one that had an impact on the proposed MHSA program design, was that 60 percent of all 1991 MHSA claims were for adolescents.

Other analyses by diagnostic categories showed the growth in hospital costs for MHSA cases between 1990 and 1991. As indicated in Figure 5.1, inpatient costs for MHSA were significantly higher than for any other diagnostic category and higher in 1991 than in 1990.

The "Carve-Out" Decision

Clearly, MHSA care required some kind of management but, the question was, *what kind?* After much discussion, Alcan decided that MHSA care would become a network-based comprehensive integrated employee assistance and managed mental health pilot program—the first step toward the introduction of managed care for all medical services. Medical care, on the other hand, would continue to be provided under the existing (that is, 1992) plan design but with the introduction of precertification and concurrent review for hospital care.

After several weeks of consultation and with many refinements, Alcan approved a new MHSA benefit plan that reversed the previous incentives toward inpatient locus of care (see Table 5.3).

The plan provides coverage for many innovative, in-network benefit options. The point-of-service design provides in- and out-of-network choices as well as centralized triage by the managed care vendor. The plan covers all

Table 5.2. Paid Claims Experience at Alcan (1990–1991)

	Percentage Change
Total medical claims	+29.1
MHSA claims	+46.9
Covered employees	−0.9
Approximate covered lives	−0.9
MHSA cost per employee	+48.2

**Figure 5.1. 1990–1991 Inpatient Services,
Amount Paid by Diagnostic Category**

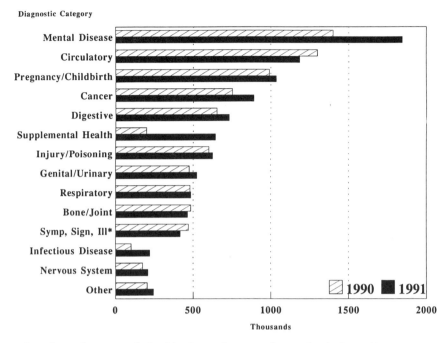

salaried employees and eligible dependents in the medical plan; EAP services are also extended to salaried employees who are not in the medical plan.

For ease of administration, MHSA is carved out of the medical plan. As a result, the deductibles, out-of-pocket maximums, and lifetime limits are separate from those for medical care. In addition, all out-of-network inpatient care must be precertified by the mental health vendor; otherwise, there is a noncompliance penalty. The vendor selection process was started early in 1992, with a two-phase approach to implementation of the MHSA program. In phase 1, the selected specialty MHSA vendor (U.S. Behavioral Health [USBH]), in midyear, introduced precertification, concurrent review, discharge planning, and catastrophic case management for all inpatient and alternative levels of care. This was instituted without changing the existing MHSA plan design. Phase 2 began on January 1, 1993, when Alcan implemented the comprehensive integrated EAP and managed MHSA point-of-service program. At that time, the redesigned MHSA benefits were instituted and carved out of the medical plan, and a national EAP program was introduced. Claims payment for both in-network and out-of-network claims are done by USBH.

In summary, Alcan saw this program as an opportunity to standardize its EAPs across the nation, close the gap in the benefit package by equalizing

Table 5.3. Managed Mental Health/Substance Abuse Point-of-Service Plan Design at Alcan

Provision	In-Network	Out-of-Network
Annual deductible	None	$200 per person
Out-of-pocket maximum	$700 per person, $1,400 per family per calendar year	$5,000 per person per calendar year; excludes deductible
Inpatient		
Mental health	90% with UR	60% with UR, 45 days per year
Substance abuse	90% with UR; 2 episodes per lifetime (reduced to 1 episode if 1 out-of-network episode used)	60% with UR; 30 days per year, 1 episode per lifetime
Intermediate care	100%	70% with UR
Outpatient		
Mental health	100%, with $15 copayment	50% after deductible; up to 25 visits per year; not subject to out of pocket (OOP)
Substance abuse	100%, with $15 copayment	50% after deductible; up to 25 visits per year; not subject to OOP
In-home mental health	100% with case management	Not available
Drug testing as an adjunct to substance abuse treatment	100% with case management	Not available
Maximum lifetime benefit (mental health and substance abuse)	$250,000 combined; 2 in-patient substance abuse treatment episodes per lifetime	$125,000 combined; 1 in-patient substance abuse treatment episode per lifetime
Eligibility	Same as medical plan	Immediate for full-time employees; 1-year waiting period for eligible dependents during first year of the program
Preexisting conditions	Same as medical plan	Same as medical plan
Provider eligibility	Full panel (M.D., Ph.D., M.S.W., M.A.)	M.D., Ph.D. clinical psychologist only

coverage for medical and MHSA care, enhance the overall quality of MHSA services, and pilot a managed care program in a discrete subspecialty to test employee acceptance and help acclimate them to future changes in the administration of their health benefits. Figures 5.2 and 5.3 show how EAP services are linked to the network-based MHSA program. Those Alcan companies with existing EAPs can retain them and establish linkages to the MHSA program (Figure 5.2), or they can elect to implement the integrated EAP/managed care program provided by USBH (Figure 5.3). Eligible employees in companies without existing EAPs are included in the integrated EAP/MHSA program.

Design of Alcan's MHSA Program

In designing a comprehensive MHSA program, Alcan wanted to make certain that the program would be consistent with their benefit objectives. The following additional goals were identified specifically for the managed MHSA program: provide a benefit that would include a continuum of care options; improve the quality of care by reducing overutilization of hospitals; reduce the per-employee MHSA cost; manage and enhance the effectiveness of inpatient and outpatient care; expand and redefine the role of EAPS, ensuring that a uniform, high-quality EAP benefit is offered to all salaried employees; and provide innovative, cost-effective care programs for adolescents. With these additional objectives in mind, Alcan began to develop specifications and standards for the program and for a point-of-service benefit plan design. They were grouped into five major categories: general considerations, provider network, access, utilization management, and member services.

**Figure 5.2. Company with Existing EAP
Linked to Managed Care Program**

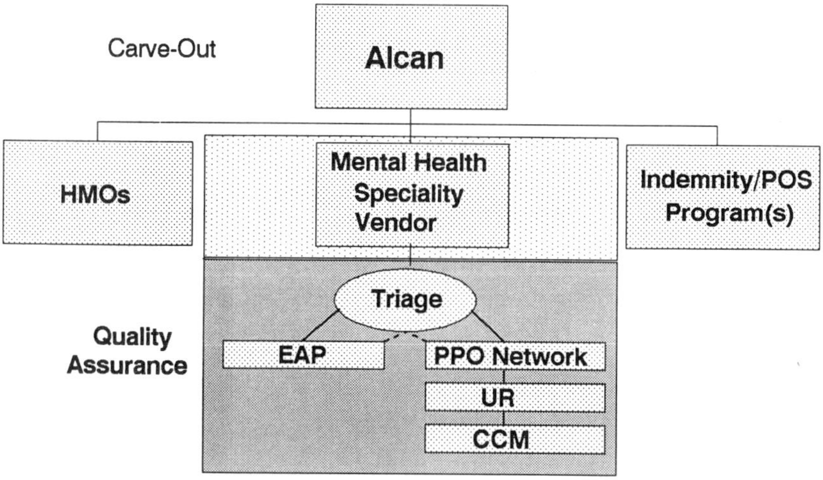

Figure 5.3. Company with Integrated EAP/Managed Care Program

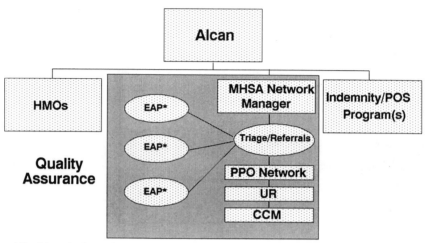

* Provide evaluation and assessment.

The most important considerations for selecting a vendor were the existence of a sound, clinically based formal process for referring patients to the appropriate level of care and formal case dispositions once admission or treatment was initiated. Due to the large number of inpatient adolescent admissions, it was important to Alcan that the vendor have procedures and standards that would foster movement from inpatient care (when necessary) to less restrictive, clinically appropriate alternatives and outpatient care wherever possible. Alcan also wanted a vendor that demonstrated skilled, specialized case management of adolescent patients. In addition, reporting was important. Alcan required high-quality quarterly and annual reporting of network performance against selected quality, administrative, and cost-effectiveness standards.

Approximately 50 percent of Alcan's employee population is dispersed into groups of fewer than one hundred people, a number of them in rural areas. Alcan was therefore interested in the vendor's approach to the development and characteristics of the provider network. Alcan specified a multi-disciplinary panel of mental health professionals, including M.D.'s, Ph.D.'s, M.S.W.'s, M.A. psychotherapists, and a sufficient selection of specialty practitioners and facilities. Credentialing of these practitioners was to be rigorous and comprehensive and include stringent criteria as well as verification of credentialing and training. In addition, the vendor was required to indicate how high-quality providers and facilities would be identified for employees in rural areas where there was no existing network and one would not likely be developed. These practitioners and facilities in rural areas would be held to the same standards and credentialing requirements as others. Employees in these areas would receive the same in-network benefit coverage and case management services as others who live in areas with a dense network of contracted providers.

Access, both to network providers and telephonically to clinicians at the vendor's centralized location, was important. Alcan required a clinical referral line to be available twenty-four hours a day, seven days a week, with specific procedures to handle emergency calls during and after regular office hours. Provider access was specified as follows:

Network mental health outpatient services must be within a twenty- to thirty-minute drive for 80 percent of the employees.

Network inpatient facilities and alternative twenty-four-hour facilities must be within one hour's drive from the employee's residence or work site.

Routine initial outpatient mental health or substance abuse visits must be available within seventy-two hours, urgent initial outpatient visits within twenty-four hours, and emergency outpatient visits immediately.

For utilization review, Alcan specified mandatory precertification for both in- and out-of-network inpatient and alternative care admissions. Mandatory precertification for initial outpatient treatment was not required, but a call for a referral to a network provider in order to receive in-network benefits, as well as a concurrent review at every tenth visit for in-network outpatient care, were required.

Alcan specified at least one case manager per 30,000 to 40,000 employees for inpatients and one case manager per 60,000 to 100,000 employees for outpatients. In addition, catastrophic case management would need to be provided so that the patient would be followed from the beginning to the end of treatment. Alcan also required a case management system that would be proactive and target for management any patient meeting one of the following "red flag" criteria: is an adolescent, exceeds a cost of $15,000, is a second inpatient admission within one year, or is a dual diagnosis (medical/mental health, medical/substance abuse, or mental health/substance abuse).

The customer service requirements included a dedicated unit or representative to answer inquiries about eligibility, claims processing, and claims payment; answering calls from members within twenty seconds; a call abandonment rate of less than 4 percent; call monitoring; and staffing levels of one member services representative per 8,000 Alcan enrollees.

A well-developed quality assurance program was also required, one that included internal staff training and external training for providers, as well as a random record review process. In addition, explicit protocols for handling complaints and a formal grievance procedure were mandatory. The initial plan design and program specifications were reviewed during a meeting held with senior human resource managers representing all major Alcan operating companies. Alcan incorporated their suggestions and concerns into the plan design prior to the request for proposal that was sent out to the vendors selected to bid.

Summary of the Process

This comprehensive approach may be unusual for a company of Alcan's size. Clearly, it is a progressive, thorough, and multilevel strategy that did the following: recognized the cost impact and quality-of-care defects in the previous benefit plans; was ready to manage the medical plans, especially the MHSA benefit plan; used a careful diagnostic approach, including data analysis, plan design review, and input from many constituencies; developed a custom-designed program, bid, and vendor selection process; avoided shifting costs to employees; kept benefit levels adequate; kept employees satisfied; recognized that employees can be under stress and offered a way to provide assistance; and creatively addressed the increasing diversity in the workforce.

Lessons Learned

Three key factors can be identified from Alcan's experience thus far:
• The design and implementation of an organized system of care can and should be compatible with and an extension of a company's health care philosophy. If an interpretation or refinement of this philosophy is needed to be certain that it is in harmony with the culture of the organization, the challenge is to communicate it to employees in the context of the company's philosophy and history.
• Building consensus is very important—holding meetings, providing information, soliciting input, and continuing a dialogue with the goal of informing key managers and others in all operating units and reporting on progress. This helps prevent people from feeling that managed care is a "knee-jerk" response based on financial factors alone.
• Paying attention to implementation is important. This includes the following measures:

Being sensitive to and developing careful plans for patients and clients currently in treatment. Communicating provisions for continuity of care, including continuity with one's existing therapist.
Addressing program-specific issues to establish adequate linkages between prior carriers and administrators and the new vendors.
Including the existing EAPs for clarification of roles and responsibilities and developing procedures to co-manage cases and handle joint referrals.
Training the trainers so that implementation issues and employee communication can be uniformly and completely addressed at local levels.

Last but not least, it is important to remember that a successful program introduction is only the first step. Alcan has committed itself to a continuing process of communication and employee education, so that both the company and its employees can reap the full benefits of these managed MHSA programs.

LAURA ALTMAN, Ph.D., board certified and trained in psychology and mental health economics, is a consultant in Towers Perrin's Boston office and former clinical director of a private, multiservice mental health agency.

WENDY PRICE, M.B.A., is manager, medical benefits, for Alcan Aluminum Corporation in Cleveland, Ohio.

It is both possible and essential to control care for public patients
so as to improve care and avoid further erosion of services
by utilizing community resources.

Managed Mental Health Care in the Public Sector

David Dangerfield, Rod L. Betit

Countless publications and conferences have been devoted to discussions of the changing behavioral health care world. Many have called these changes a revolution in how behavioral health services are being delivered. One significant change has been the development of risk-based managed care. Managed care for mental health and substance abuse services is now prevalent in privately funded health benefit plans; it is, however, relatively new to public sector payors.

A number of factors impel government policy makers to experiment with alternative health care delivery systems: an increasing need to control costs; the need to ensure adequate access for a rapidly increasing Medicaid population; frequent positive reports from the private sector about the success of methods that shift more of the financial risk to the provider; a conviction that providers should be much more conscious of treatment outcomes and have a greater ability to justify the expenditure of public money for mental health services; positive experiences with other Medicaid-managed care projects (HMOs, alternatives to nursing home care, and so on); and recognition that better, more cost-effective treatment options exist but cannot be utilized unless the paradigm for treatment is changed.

Utah's Prepaid Mental Health Plan

On July 1, 1991, the Utah Medicaid Prepaid Mental Health Plan was implemented in three areas of the state. The plan allows contractors, selected by the state through a request-for-proposal process, to deliver all needed mental health services to all the Medicaid recipients in their geographic area. The contractor can provide the service or can subcontract with other providers. In the first two years of the plan, the contractor is at risk for all inpatient but at no risk for outpatient psychiatric services. With the start of the third year, the contractor is at full financial risk for all services.

In order for the program to be implemented, the Utah State Medicaid Agency needed approval from the Health Care Financing Administration (HCFA) for a 1915(b) Freedom of Choice Waiver. Under the waiver, Medicaid-eligible people in certain geographic areas are required to obtain mental health services, inpatient and outpatient, through a single entity that has contracted with the state. The initial waiver period runs for two years.

All mental health services are included—inpatient and related physician services and outpatient services provided both on and off the clinic site. The benefits include evaluation and assessment; psychological testing; individual, group, and family therapy; medication management; day treatment; and targeted case management for the chronically mentally ill. All Medicaid enrollees are included in the plan, with the exception of those who are in the Utah State Hospital.

Valley Mental Health (VMH), one of the three demonstration sites, is a private, not-for-profit organization that contracts with a number of organizations to provide mental health and substance abuse services. In the State of Utah, the elected county commissioners serve as the local mental health authority and, as such, are responsible for public mental health services in each county. VMH has contracted with Salt Lake and Summit counties, as well as with various state agencies, educational systems, and correctional agencies, to provide mental health services. In addition, VMH also contracts with private insurance companies and employer groups, at risk, under managed care arrangements.

The annual operating budget of VMH is $36 million, the staff numbers over 600, and the catchment area has a population of 750,000 (44 percent of the population of Utah). Within this population, approximately 48,000 are enrolled in the Medicaid program.

Capitation: Crucial Elements

Like many private capitation arrangements, this Medicaid demonstration project has the following key elements:

Care is prepaid. VMH receives, on a monthly basis, a prepaid sum to cover the cost of providing all necessary care as well as administrative costs. This payment is, in effect, a premium for each person on Medicaid who lives in the designated area. The premium is a combination of two rates: (1) inpatient hospital and related physician services, and (2) all outpatient mental health clinic services. There is a different premium rate for each of the eligible categories in the Medicaid program, reflecting age, disability, and risk factors. VMH is not paid for the services provided but instead receives an agreed-on amount for each person enrolled in the Medicaid population.

Provider at financial risk. In years 1 and 2, VMH is at full financial risk only for the inpatient hospital and physician services, not for outpatient services. There will be a cost settlement at the end of each year based on the actual number of services provided for outpatients. In year 3, both the inpatient and physician services and the outpatient services will be at full financial risk to VMH. This arrangement will be explained later.

Incentive to manage care wisely. In this project, as in any capitated managed care program, the provider of services has a financial incentive to manage care wisely. Three critical elements are taken into account:

• Access. How available should the treatment be? The provider must consider access in terms of not only geography and availability, but also the criteria that may be used to determine eligibility for services (that is, diagnosis, severity ratings, and so on). The more accessible the service, the higher the costs. On the other hand, if access is limited, care will probably be compromised.

• Quality of Care. One of the major criticisms leveled against managed health care is that quality of care is compromised. Although this criticism may or may not be justified, the provider of service must continually guard against allowing financial incentives to drive treatment decisions. On the positive side, it is possible that these same financial incentives can stimulate innovation and improvements in the quality of care.

• Quantity. A challenge to all managed health care providers is to determine the optimal amount of service for any given individual. Too often in mental health services, it is the clinician's background, practice traditions, and therapeutic bias that drive these decisions. In a managed mental health system, it is a continual balancing act to ensure appropriate access, optimum quantity, and quality of care. Not enough care or too much care can have devastating effects on a client.

Payments tied to a specific risk pool. Capitation payments are always tied to a specific risk pool. Despite the increasing shift toward managed care in the private sector, movement toward this model has generally been slow in public programs. Much of the hesitation is because of the perception that the Medicaid population is a greater risk than private sector employees.

Some of the enrollees in the Medicaid population are there because of their mental health disability. This implies, of course, that they are the severely and persistent mentally ill. Balancing the care for this population across the variables of access, quality, and quantity has challenged mental health providers for a long time. Furthermore, many children and youth are enrolled in Medicaid because they are in the custody of the state. This is frequently a result of failure on the part of their natural support systems to provide for their basic needs, either through neglect, abandonment, or abuse. These conditions cause severe emotional scarring that often requires intensive mental health intervention. Others in the Medicaid population are there because of difficult financial circumstances.

It can easily be argued that this population generally requires a more intensive and broader array of mental health treatment services than others. And

yet, within the Medicaid population, while there are some extremely high utilizers of mental health services, there are many who do not use any. VMH's experience to date is that 13 percent of the overall Medicaid population and 40
percent of the disabled Medicaid population use mental health services.

Motivation of the Funding Agent

It is critical in the development of any managed care program, particularly
working with a public payor, that the provider understand the unique characteristics of the environment within which the managed care program will be operating. In such an assessment, the motivation of the funding agent is critical.

In Utah, there has been a tremendous growth in the cost of mental
health inpatient services, primarily for children and adolescents. Prior to the
implementation of the managed care program, the state Medicaid agency put
into place an in-house utilization and review program in an attempt to control costs. This helped, but it was decided that a second cost containment
step was needed. As a result, a diagnostic related group (DRG) payment
method was implemented. Although this program did help contain costs, it
did not allow for the development of community-based alternatives to inpatient care. Thus, the next logical step was managed care. The need to gain
more control over the growth in number and cost of inpatient mental health
services was a predominant theme in the discussions between the state
Medicaid agency and VMH.

In December 1984, Utah's Certificate of Need Program expired. With no
approved process for hospital bed expansion, the way was paved for a dramatic increase in psychiatric bed capacity. Between 1984 and 1987, eight
new freestanding psychiatric facilities opened. At the same time, acute care
hospitals with psychiatric wings also increased their number of beds. Within
three years, psychiatric beds in the state more than doubled—from 784 in
1984 to 1,623 in 1987.

The state Medicaid agency recognized that, under a fee-for-service
model, there was a strong bias toward intensive services. Medicaid paid for
acute inpatient care directly to a variety of hospitals, each operating their
own psychiatric units. It was found, however, that there was little coordination of care with outpatient services. On the other hand, the community
mental health center and other private providers were supplying outpatient
mental health services, primarily to children, but with no particular financial
incentive to coordinate care with inpatient providers. Furthermore, alternatives to inpatient care such as residential treatment and supported housing
options were not reimbursable by Medicaid under a fee-for-service program.

Payor and Provider Expected Outcomes

If a provider assumes increased financial risk through managed care, it is
necessary to work in partnership with the payor. The more the financial risk

is shifted from payor to provider, the greater the need for a real partnership that begins with an agreement about objectives and outcomes. If the payor is only interested in cost containment, there is no basis for a true partnership. There must also be a desire to improve the quality of care.

In the Utah model, VMH and the Medicaid agency formulated at the outset specific objectives that were to be accomplished by moving from fee-for-service to managed care:

Cost containment. The development of a financing mechanism to obtain real cost containment was a major incentive for the funding agency. In the development of the project, it was clear that long-term cost containment could be achieved, but, in the initial stages, there would be an increase in the cost of outpatient services. Inpatient costs would be reduced and outpatient costs increased for the first two years to guarantee sufficient resources to develop a complete community-based continuum of care. Only by having a full continuum of services could clients be provided care that would meet their needs. In Utah, under the fee-for-service model, there was not a fully developed service continuum; this was particularly true for children and adolescents. It was felt that if inpatient cost containment could be achieved in years 1 and 2, it could be phased in on the outpatient side and the third year would produce total cost containment.

Flexibility in resource management. Flexibility in managing treatment resources was critical to this project. It was important for the provider to be able to use treatment programs that, in the past, would not be reimbursed under Medicaid fee-for-service. Residential treatment, room-and-board arrangements, and supported housing programs needed to be developed if hospital utilization was to be lowered. Under the capitated program, the provider is able to purchase or provide those services that best meet client needs, thus ensuring real quality with reduced costs.

This has been an exciting part of the capitated program. VMH has developed new programs for both children and adults. The child programs now include after-school day treatment. Traditionally, the day treatment programs have had a school component, but now there is a new day treatment program that enables us to keep children connected to their community-based schools when possible.

Focused accountability. In a managed care program, the provider is accountable for three major areas: (1) expenditure of funds, (2) administration, and (3) service delivery and coordination of care. This is different from a fee-for-service model, where the provider is only responsible for the specific services rendered. The more focused and centralized the accountability for all aspects of care, the more likely the quality of care is to improve.

Innovation and improvement in community-based care. Mental health services can be improved by having both the flexibility and the motivation to foster innovations in community-based treatment. Under the Utah demonstration project, one of the innovative strategies developed was for VMH to contract with the child welfare system. The child welfare agency provides, on behalf of VMH, intensive in-home services. For years, the child welfare agency and its staff developed strategies and technologies in family crisis management. Those skills can now be used to assist the mental health provider in ensuring appropriate care for younger Medicaid clients. The joint ownership has improved community relations and continuity of care for a difficult population.

A second example of how the financing mechanism of this managed care project can foster innovation is the method developed to utilize treatment settings that have traditionally not been included in the Medicaid fee-for-service financing. Treatment settings that have been labeled *institutions for mental disease* (IMDs) had been excluded from Medicaid reimbursement. Many high-quality and less expensive freestanding psychiatric facilities and residential treatment programs are classified as such. Under the managed care program, the client can receive care best offered by an IMD. VMH's use of some of these programs has allowed movement from hospital, residential, or day treatment to outpatient care in a much smoother and more effective manner.

Service flexibility. Since providers no longer need to be concerned about whether they are going to be reimbursed for a specific service, they can plan a configuration of services uniquely tailored to the individual. Under a capitated system, providers must think critically about the quantity of the services they are providing. Services are an expense rather than additional revenue. The fee-for-service model has built-in incentives for the mental health provider to create dependency in the clientele. The opposite is true in a managed care system.

These changed financial incentives have the potential to improve the quality of care. This is particularly true with the chronic and severely mentally ill. VMH's acute day treatment program is an example of this. In the past, day treatment was seen as mostly long term. With the incentive of cost containment and the flexibility of capitation, intensive short-term day treatment as a hospital diversion has become a reality. To date, only one client referred into the program has not successfully avoided a hospital admission.

Reduced reporting requirements. It is also possible under this system to reduce reporting requirements. There is less need in managed care for highly specific reporting and medical chart compliance requirements; one of the major complaints by professional staff in the public sector is the overwhelming burden of paperwork. Cost-based retrospective audits that require a tremendous amount of time and energy in the fee-for-service model are eliminated in managed care. The focus now is to make the treatment plan and documentation a working part of the overall treatment. The goal is to make it relevant to the clients' treatment, instead of an exercise for reimbursement purposes.

Cost savings to enhance other services. The savings from managed care can be used to enhance other services. As the provider is able to develop service and cost efficiencies, the financial savings can go to the provider's bottom line. "Going to the bottom line" in this instance means that VMH is able to take any dollars saved in the capitated portion of the Medicaid program and underwrite services to other mentally ill but primarily indigent individuals. When operating a public mental health agency, there never seems to be enough money to meet the ever-growing needs and severity of problems. Agency after agency is looking at ways to raise funds and increase other charitable activities. If one can be efficient in the capitated Medicaid program, the dollars saved can legitimately be used to underwrite other important activities.

Areas of Concern

In any pilot or experimental project, there are potential gains as well as losses. To date, the experience in this project suggests that there has been an overall improvement in quality of care and cost efficiencies. However, because there is a large financial risk, as well as many unpredictable elements in dealing with the Medicaid population, certain concerns must be continually monitored:

Does the potential for savings really exist? VMH's experience indicates yes. This project is in an environment where rapid increases in inpatient costs have occurred, particularly for children and adolescents. Thus, great opportunities existed to reduce hospital lengths of stay as well as to provide alternatives to hospital admissions. The goal of VMH at the inception of this project was that one out of every ten adults who requested an inpatient admission be placed in an appropriate alternative to hospitalization and that the average length of stay for all adults be reduced by two days. With regard to the child and adolescent population, the goal was that appropriate alternatives would be found for two out of every ten who requested an inpatient admission and that the average length of stay be reduced by four days. To date, these goals have been achieved, cost savings realized, and beneficial treatment alternatives provided. We have indeed been able to contain costs on the inpatient side. So far, the total inpatient cost for both adults and children has been 50 percent lower than our goal. In other projects in different environments and circumstances, the savings may differ. The Medicaid population is very needy in terms of mental health services, so that caution is required in undertaking these projects.

Will the chronically mentally ill obtain needed services? It would be unfortunate if those most in need did not obtain services because of overaggressive financial incentives that inappropriately restrict care. Just as incentives in fee-for-service models can encourage the provider to offer more care than is needed, under managed care the incentives may work to prevent needed services. The provider must be constantly alert to this possibility.

Planning for Success

As negotiations with the state Medicaid agency began prior to implementation of the project, three critical financial elements were identified as necessary for the project to be successful; these had to do with risk, rate changes, and stop-loss arrangements.

Risk. In the early planning for the capitated Medicaid program and through the course of the negotiations between VMH and the state Medicaid agency, it became evident that a complete array of community-based services for the mentally ill had not yet been developed. In fact, children's services were seriously underdeveloped, and it was likely that many of the mental health needs of children in the Medicaid population were unserved.

It seemed premature to engage in a project that would put VMH at 100 percent financial risk. The capitation payment rate of any managed care program is based primarily on the historical utilization data. To accommodate the newly covered Medicaid services and the projected unmet need, VMH projected significant Medicaid cost increases for outpatient services. The state Medicaid agency became concerned because this would be reflected in a much higher projected capitation rate than the historical utilization would suggest. Therefore, a plan was developed under which a risk and nonrisk approach to the project would be phased in to full risk over three years.

VMH currently receives a prepaid monthly amount for inpatient hospital and physician services. A separate rate exists for each of the eligibility categories within the Medicaid population. VMH is at 100 percent financial risk. If VMH pays less for inpatient services than the capitation rates it receives, it retains the difference. If, on the other hand, VMH spends more for inpatient services than it is paid, VMH is required to make up the difference. VMH also pays administrative overages, including claims processing; it also covers nontraditional services—such as foster care, short-term residential treatment, and room-and-board arrangements—that cannot be paid through traditional outpatient Medicaid funding.

On the nonrisk side, there are the traditional outpatient services that include individual, group, and family therapy; medications; day treatment; case management; and rehabilitation. A capitation rate for each of the Medicaid eligible categories is established for these, and VMH is paid at the first of each month for all Medicaid enrollees.

At the end of the first two fiscal years of the project, a retroactive settlement will be made between the nonrisk payments and the actual services provided. This means that VMH has an obligation to keep fee-for-service data on outpatient services and submit them to the Medicaid agency at the end of each of the first two fiscal years. If outpatient services provided cost more than the capitation rates paid, the state agency will pay VMH the difference at the end of each year. On the other hand, if services provided were less than the capitation rates VMH received, VMH will return the overpayment. In year 3, VMH will be at full risk for the entire plan, and capitation rates will be established for each of the eligibility categories, including inpatient, inpatient physician, and all outpatient services.

Rate changes. The second element critical to the success of the project was to develop a mechanism whereby the monthly premium rate could be changed during the course of the year. Because the Medicaid population is involved with a number of other government social service programs, a policy change in any one of them would be likely to have a direct effect on the assumptions used in setting the monthly capitation rate for mental health services. As an example, the Utah State Hospital has no formal administrative connection to the local community mental health center. It could change its policies related to access of patients. If this occurred, Medicaid recipients in need of hospital care could be denied it. This would require VMH to spend more money on acute inpatient hospitalization than had been contemplated when the original capitation rates were set.

Stop-loss arrangements. Because the capitated Medicaid program in Utah differs from other public mental health programs across the country, VMH and the state were concerned about the need to develop a form of stop-loss insurance. VMH was unable to find any insurance through the commercial market and thus developed a stop-loss arrangement in cooperation with the state Medicaid agency. VMH subtracts an amount to fund the stop-loss from the monthly paid capitation rate. This money is placed in a separate trust account held jointly by VMH and the state. At the end of the contract year, if there have been catastrophic claims in inpatient services, the trust fund can be used. After all inpatient claims are paid and settlement is made for any difference over $25,000, the state Medicaid agency and VMH split the amount of money left in the trust account according to a predetermined formula. The experience with the stop-loss to date has proved to be acceptable to both the state and VMH.

Provider Issues

In a managed care environment, providers can ensure that the recipients of service will be able to receive the care they need, when they need it. This is in contrast to the traditional fee-for-service approach, in which clients receive services that the provider gets paid for, not necessarily services that meet their needs. Managed care does not guarantee that clients get what they need, but it does provide the opportunity for this to happen. To utilize the flexibility provided by managed care, VMH developed the following principles:

Enhanced service to priority patients. The role of VMH is to serve the severely and persistently mentally ill as a first priority. Many in this category are also enrolled in the Medicaid program. Managed care allows VMH to better carry out its mandates to the highest-priority clients.

Individualized treatment planning. Clients receive professional and thorough assessment of their needs. VMH is obligated to work in partnership with the client to determine how to best meet the needs identified in the assessment process. Often the client is not so much in need of ongoing therapy or traditional forms of day treatment as of support and social skills development, education or work training opportunities, and job skill assessments.

Involvement of natural support systems. VMH continually seeks ways to develop, involve, and strengthen the natural support systems of clients. This is particularly important in working with children and adolescents.

Affordable and decent housing. Housing should offer clients the opportunity to feel a sense of independence, allow for privacy, and encourage the development of self-worth. Active support of mentally ill clients in their own housing is key to preventing hospitalization. All too frequently, acute hospitalization is precipitated by a crisis in a client's living arrangements.

Ease of access to flexible programs. Clients need to feel that there are no rigid requirements to access services. If access is made too difficult, they are more likely to allow their illness to develop to such a point that severe decompensation occurs and a much more costly and long-term hospitalization will be required. Ease of access is a preventive technique and in the long run is cost-effective.

VMH actively reaches out to clients to help them achieve maximum benefits from their treatment options. Reducing care to reduce costs is shortsighted. This is especially true in dealing with the chronically mentally ill. Active outreach may, for example, encourage an early hospitalization and prevent a more extensive hospital stay later on.

Broad array of services. It would be difficult to attempt an at-risk managed care program without all the tools necessary to provide flexible and individually tailored services. A managed mental health program must have a broad array of services, from the most to the least restrictive. VMH needs to be a mental health "shopping mall," with the ability to provide a wide variety of specialty programs.

Location of services. VMH develops relationships with homeless shelters, welfare departments, schools, correctional agencies, and the like. In this way, others can carry out their "treatment" roles with the at-risk population and bring about treatment and cost efficiencies.

VMH will have outpatient units in all geographic areas of the county in an attempt to be where the clients are. For example, a special drug and alcohol unit for the homeless is located near the homeless shelter.

Single clinical authority. It is extremely important that all clinical services be coordinated. The administrator of the managed care program must be the single-point clinical authority that can quickly resolve any disputes that occur. VMH is the central clinical authority for services rendered by other providers. This reduces the potential for clinical disputes. Ultimate financial responsibility and final clinical authority go hand in hand. In the development of the managed care program, VMH had to decide how many subcontractors there should be. It was decided to provide as many of the services in-house as possible. Outside providers are used only if they have expertise with a particular diagnostic problem or treatment that VMH does not. It is easier to manage the risk if VMH has direct control over the majority of the providers. Inpatient services are the exception, but the number of hospitals included is as limited as possible.

This limiting has evolved in many instances into a team effort between VMH and other agencies. This has allowed for some creative programs resulting from the different opinions, training, and experiences of the other participating providers.

Precertification and utilization review. A major component of the VMH managed care program is a strong precertification and utilization review process with the following key elements:

1. The precertification is done by a highly trained professional staff.

2. The review has well-defined, clearly understood criteria for each diagnostic category.

3. The client, the client's support system, and the clinician need to understand that there is a readily available second opinion process. If at any point in the precertification a disagreement or questioning of the reviewers' decision occurs, the use of a second opinion is immediately encouraged.

4. The utilization review staff has ready access to medical consultations.

5. The precertification reviewers see themselves as advocates for the clients. Clients need to feel, as the review is progressing, that the process is not intended to prevent them from receiving needed care, but to help them get what they need when they need it.

6. The precertification for hospitalization is only given for a short time, and a concurrent utilization review is in place. Concurrent reviews are done on a face-to-face basis with the client and hospital staff. On-site reviews have been found to be a key component in properly evaluating the level of care needed by the client.

Case management. Case management includes coordinating care and connecting elements of care to one another, advocating for the client to be able to get what is needed, and an ongoing monitoring system to determine the effectiveness of services.

A Case Example: How It Works for Real People

This chapter has focused on the advantage of a capitated treatment system for public mental health. Central to this demonstration project is the concept that one entity is ultimately responsible for care. In the past, care was fragmented, with little responsibility from one provider to the next for linking the various treatment interventions in a meaningful whole. The financial incentive to reduce costly inpatient care becomes a significant motivator in coordinating care. A case example will demonstrate the different approaches to treatment before and after capitation.

Billy is eleven years old and lives with his mother, two older brothers, and a younger sister. Prior to the implementation of the managed care system, he had two hospitalizations. The first was precipitated by a violent temper tantrum. After a call from Billy's mother, the welfare worker initiated hospitalization. Billy stayed in the hospital thirty-five days and then returned home. The hospital staff suggested that the mother contact the mental health center for family therapy. She made one contact, but because of transportation problems, she did not keep the appointment. The school reported that Billy's adjustment in class after his first hospitalization was poor.

Five months later, Billy's mother, being "at her wit's end," asked the welfare department how she could put Billy in a foster home. He was being defiant and abusive to his younger sister and totally lacking in school performance. She was also sure that he was responsible for several incidents of missing money in the home. The second hospitalization was precipitated after a confrontation with Billy regarding her desire to send him to a foster home. He ran away from home and was picked up by the police several hours later. They took him to the local runaway shelter. The staff described him as "extremely emotionally disturbed" and recommended hospitalization. They made arrangements for admission. He stayed forty-five days and was again returned to his mother. The recommendation was that she obtain outpatient therapy for Billy from the local mental health center. She made the contact, and he was seen on three occasions. He missed the next two appointments, and no further ones were made.

His third admission occurred after the managed Medicaid system was initiated. Seven months after Billy's second admission, his mother called her welfare worker in a distressed state. She had found him with a pocket knife cutting deep scratches on his arms. Just before this, a teacher had expressed concern regarding what she considered to be "black pictures" that he had drawn at school. The welfare worker again contacted the hospital but was told that Billy could not be admitted until Valley Mental Health had given its approval.

After hearing from the hospital, VMH sent a mobile outreach worker to Billy's home. At that initial assessment, he was approved for inpatient care. The mobile outreach worker explained that two people would be assigned to work with Billy and his family. A primary therapist in one of VMH's outpatient clinics would be an important person in helping the family plan for discharge from the hospital and would be an ongoing resource in helping Billy and the family. The family could use the second person, a case manager, for help in arranging transportation to therapy, coordinating with the school, and seeing to it that any barriers to implementing plans the family and the treatment staff developed were minimized.

This admission was for eight days. During Billy's stay, the case manager coordinated joint planning between the primary therapist, hospital staff, welfare worker, school, and family. They developed a treatment plan for Billy's discharge to include placement in a day treatment program that met three hours every day after school. He was in this program for six weeks.

The day treatment program is operated by VMH and has been specially designed to accommodate latency-age children in coordination with schools. Assistance with class assignments given in the regular school was provided by the day treatment staff on a daily basis. This link between school and day treatment was kept current with the assistance of the case manager. The program supplied transportation.

Family therapy was provided by the primary therapist, who consulted regularly with day treatment staff. In addition, through the case manager, VMH arranged for the welfare department to provide crisis outreach in the home. These crisis interventions by the welfare department were paid for by VMH.

It has been fourteen months since Billy's last admission. The family reports significant improvement in their home life. Billy appears happier and is performing better in school than he has for several years. Facilitating family therapy and coordinating care from a central point seemed to be the key. This is in direct contrast to the fragmented approach evidenced in the first two hospitalizations.

Resistance to Managed Care

In implementing the managed care project, private providers, advocates, and VMH staff raised a number of concerns. VMH, like many community mental health centers, had become somewhat institutionalized. Some clients were not getting what they needed but rather what the staff knew how or wanted to provide, or even more important, what the organization would be paid for under the traditional fee-for-service model.

A particular concern of many VMH staff was the necessity under the managed care system to have an "outsider" be responsible for the precertification and utilization review. In the private sector, many private clinicians had grown accustomed to being monitored. This has not necessarily been part of the tradition of community mental health centers. As the Medicaid capitated program began, the staff were concerned that the reviewers would be challenging their commitment and their long-standing history of work with the mentally ill. It was suggested to them that the new program would require accountability but would provide more flexibility, more innovation, and improvement in continuity of care.

Summary

Due to strong market forces and payor concerns, first in the private and now in the public sector, the mental health field is changing. The survivors and leaders will be the innovators and risk takers. They must have the ability to look critically at themselves and make needed changes. This new environment creates great opportunity to provide better mental health care.

Capitated mental health programs for Medicaid beneficiaries are developing in various forms across the country, and mental health providers, both private and public, need to be aware of those developments. Such programs have great promise for community mental health centers. Medicaid is generally a major funding source for the community mental health system, and public funds should be used to the best extent possible. Managed care has great promise for cost containment and can provide financial stability for community mental health centers. The most important promise of managed care, however, is improving access to and quality of mental health services for the Medicaid population.

David Dangerfield, D.S.W., is executive director of Valley Mental Health, a private, not-for-profit organization.

Rod L. Betit is executive director of the Utah Department of Health.

*Progressive private psychiatric hospitals are moving toward providing
a full spectrum of alternative services on and off campus.*

Managed Care: A Provider Perspective

Doyle Carson

During the past several years, providers of private psychiatric care have experienced unprecedented changes. To understand these changes, one must
remember that as recently as the 1960s, access to mental health care was
quite limited. There were an inadequate number of providers, a limited
number of private psychiatric hospitals, and sparse reimbursement for psychiatric treatment. It was difficult to find child and adolescent outpatient
and inpatient services as well as other specialized services. The public sector
was overburdened, and the private sector was poorly developed.

As practitioners and the general public became more aware of the
prevalence of mental illness, it was clear that serious problems existed concerning access to care. The estimated economic cost to society of alcohol and
drug problems and mental illness was high, and treatment was often not
available. Convincing arguments were developed for better private insurance
coverage. Healthy economic times created a generally positive atmosphere,
and so the case for better coverage carried the day. Improved reimbursement
for psychiatric treatment coincided with advancing therapeutic techniques
and decreasing stigma. The stage was set for improved access to care.

Growth of Psychiatric Hospitals

In time, access was improved, but it gave way to almost uncontrollable
growth in the cost of psychiatric care. For-profit investor organizations developed to provide capital to meet the needs of psychiatric hospitals—the
new growth industry. Hospitals grew at an extraordinary rate. In the 1980s,
many states dismantled certificate-of-need laws and agencies; where this occurred, the regulatory oversight of psychiatric hospitals ceased to exist and

growth was explosive. Freestanding private psychiatric hospitals increased sevenfold in some communities. Conversion of general hospital beds to psychiatric beds was also considerable.

The growth of psychiatric hospital beds was accompanied by aggressive advertising and marketing by a number of large investor-owned companies. The psychiatric atmosphere took on a "Wall Street go-go" tone, reaching its peak in the late 1980s. Increasingly, leadership in the psychiatric hospital field was assumed by marketing and business people as enormous investments were put at risk in the psychiatric industry. Competition intensified among providers as more and more hospitals were built. Innovative marketing techniques were developed to fill hospital beds. Criticisms that patients were being admitted on the basis of "greed, not need" began to surface. With the proliferation of hospital beds, expenses associated with mental health care were escalating. Accusations of overutilization of psychiatric inpatient beds continued to grow.

Cost rather than access to psychiatric care came to be seen as the major problem in the psychiatric field, and payors became alarmed. They responded in a variety of ways: higher patient cost sharing, benefit limitations, and managed care. Because many companies have reported successful cost containment with managed care approaches, the field continues to grow.

Advent of Managed Care

The first issue that mental health providers must address is that managed care is a reality and will be with us for some time. Many do not yet accept that fact. They need to understand why managed care developed and the powerful forces behind it. One way to think about managed care is that it is the voice of the payor. Payors will no longer be left out of decisions that are costly to them. The need in our society for the development of profitable businesses and the creation of jobs is strong; containment of health care costs is one element in achieving that goal. Health care costs, including mental health costs, will be contained at some level.

With finite funding available for mental health care, attention is increasingly focused on methods of delivering treatment that balance quality and cost containment. Managed care companies have grown because of the intense need for cost containment. Their survival will depend on their ability to balance quality and cost of care. The same survival strategy holds true for providers.

A major theme that runs through the clinical philosophies of virtually all managed care companies is a shift in focus from inpatient to outpatient care. The growth of managed care is having a powerful impact on providers of treatment, especially hospitals, because of this shift. The resulting decreased lengths of stay are reducing the inpatient census of psychiatric hospitals across the country. Inpatient revenues have been so drastically curtailed that a downsizing of the psychiatric hospital industry became inevitable. The field is overbedded for the available reimbursement. Some psychiatric hospitals have closed, and others will in the next few years —perhaps as many as 50 percent. Consequently, this is a period of extreme turmoil and instability. It is a painful transition to a new era of treatment, one that emphasizes nonacute hospital alternatives.

While hospital care will continue to be an essential part of comprehensive psychiatric treatment, the role of the hospital is being redefined. It is increasingly used to stabilize patients in crisis, to provide certain special services, and to provide treatment to a small percentage of patients resistant to outpatient care. The transition to a smaller number of hospitals and beds is not easy. But once made, the psychiatric field will tend to stabilize again.

In addition to forcing a decrease in the number of inpatient beds, managed care is changing attitudes about briefer therapies. For most patients, psychiatric treatment on both an inpatient and an outpatient basis is of shorter duration than previously. Providers who are interested and who develop expertise in briefer treatments will find abundant opportunities in the future. Those who cannot or are unwilling to make the shift to briefer treatments will struggle and lament a past era.

Managed mental health is also leading to organized systems of care with a true spectrum of treatment options. Briefer hospital stays do not work without high-quality, intensive partial hospital and outpatient services. Increasingly, mental health professionals belong to organized systems that provide a continuum of treatment. The trend is toward fewer solo practitioners and more group practices.

The changes in locus of care, number of psychiatric inpatient beds, treatment attitudes about briefer therapies, and evolving organized systems of care are dramatic for providers of psychiatric treatment. The forces behind these changes are powerful, and continuing change is inevitable. For some providers, the transition is painful and represents a loss of what, for them, were highly valued treatments. For others, the future beckons with broad opportunities to develop new treatment approaches and to demonstrate that psychiatric care can be both beneficial and cost-effective.

Mistakes are and will be made. As the transition to briefer treatments proceeds, it is essential that modifications be made to correct deficiencies as they appear. Many questions need to be answered, such as the following: What treatments work? How do we measure positive outcome? How costly are treatments? Are there cost offsets? What is the effect of managed care on access? On quality? On accountability?

From a provider perspective, managed care has brought dramatic changes to the psychiatric field. These changes will continue. One positive aspect is that psychatric care of the future has a better chance than ever to demonstrate its cost-effectiveness and high quality. Our attempts to prove this will be watched closely by both consumers of and payors for care.

Timberlawn: A Case Illustration

A detailed case example will shed additional light on the points just made.

Initial Problems. The leadership of Timberlawn Psychiatric Hospital in Dallas made a decision in 1988 to move into managed care as a provider. We anticipated changes in mental health services with a likely emphasis on managed care in the future. This was a major shift in direction for Timberlawn. It came at a time when the hospital census was high and the apparent need to make such a shift into managed care was not yet clear or compelling. Accordingly, there was considerable internal resistance to the change and concern about quality of care and the harmful influences of utilization review. However, a managed care philosophy was developed on a number of inpatient units, day hospital programs were put into place, and several outpatient clinics were organized in the Dallas community to improve access to outpatient services. Marketing efforts were directed at signing managed care contracts, and movement into this type of delivery system was put into place with considerable energy and intensity.

Timberlawn's entry into the managed care arena occurred at a time when managed care was emerging in the Dallas area, and our managed care program benefited from this trend. Outpatient clinic services grew, more patients utilized outpatient services, and increasing numbers of patients were admitted to the hospital for brief inpatient stays. The average length of stay for managed care patients in the hospital began to settle at nine to ten days for adults and thirteen to fourteen days for children and adolescents. This was about 50 percent of what it had been a few years earlier.

Change in Staff Attitudes. The managed care focus forced a number of changes in the way care was provided in the hospital. Attitudes changed toward patients and their lengths of stay in the hospital. The hospital was viewed as the beginning of treatment. Most of the treatment—including day treatment—would take place on an outpatient basis, and the hospital was being redefined as a place where stabilization could occur and help make a patient safe so that outpatient therapy could be effective. Everything in a patient's inpatient program had to be done faster. Intake histories needed to be dictated and typed more quickly. Psychological testing, family involvement, and individualized treatment programs had to be put into place more rapidly. This change in the pace of treatment activity was overwhelming for some professional staff, who met it with great criticism and resistance. Despite extensive discussions, many simply could not enthusiastically support this change.

It became clear that clinicians who were going to be able to work successfully in managed care would have to enthusiastically embrace all its aspects as well as the new pace of treatment in the hospital setting. It was not constructive for a psychiatrist to admit and discharge a patient within a nine- or ten-day period while feeling cynical about the entire process, or to train psychiatric residents in the new managed care program and lament the "good old days" when patients got high-quality care rather than what was now occurring.

Members of the medical staff and other professional staff departments had to become supportive toward managed care or make room for those who would be. Accordingly, there was staff turnover as this adjustment was made in attitudes, hospital practices, and pace of treatment. This was painful, because all members of the professional staff were highly valued at Timberlawn and it was not easy to see anyone leave. Yet it was clear that a number of people would have to go in order to make the transition to a new type of hospital and outpatient care. The leadership of the hospital felt that there was no turning back: managed care would continue to grow and a professional staff would have to be developed that could enthusiastically provide such care.

Tension with utilization reviewers was another area of early concern. Managed care involves utilization review professionals overseeing the work of the hospital staff. Part of the time, the utilization review relationship worked beautifully, but on other occasions, serious problems developed. Horrendous stories were told about outrageous comments that utilization reviewers were said to have made. In return, feedback from utilization review professionals pointed out alleged comments made by our professional staff that were considered to be inappropriate and, at times, unprofessional.

Some of the greatest difficulty occurred around patients with major depressions and borderline personality disorders. The reviewers would often feel that the professional staff at the hospital was giving in to the manipulations of the patient and fostering regressive behavior. The medical staff, on the other hand, felt that many utilization review professionals were recommending approaches that were unsafe and likely to lead to psychological and physical harm to the patient. Occasionally, patients would get caught in this struggle.

The logistics of utilization review were often problematic for the medical staff. Neither the utilization review professionals nor the hospital medical staff were readily available for phone contact. At times, the utilization review professional might be available between 1:30 and 2:30 in the afternoon, Eastern time. Yet, when called, the hospital medical staff person might get a phone recording device and be asked to leave a message, call back, or wait. Utilization review professionals would complain that members of the medical staff were difficult to reach and would not return phone calls.

It became apparent after much discussion about the problems that if we had to, we could develop a number of ways to ensure that utilization review would not work. What we needed to do, however, was to make it work. This is a fundamental decision that any hospital medical staff must make if they are going to be successfully involved in managed care—to focus on how to make the new system work rather than complain about why it does not.

Our medical staff began to invite utilization reviewers to meetings, to air differences of opinion and work on solutions rather than simply focus on problems. We learned that utilization review worked more effectively when reviewers could be perceived as real people, human beings doing an important job and not simply a mechanical voice denying treatment. Gradually, the ability of the Timberlawn medical staff to work effectively with utilization review improved considerably. Problems still occur, as they always will with such issues. But solutions are now found more rapidly, and there is a more positive interaction between the hospital medical staff and the utilization reviewers.

Administrative Issues. Another set of problems faced by Timberlawn had to do with administrative issues such as information systems, collection of copayments, and personnel assignments for patient care. We had developed several comprehensive mental health clinics throughout the Dallas area, and, as a result, our mental health system was large and complex. It was necessary for one clinic to be able to communicate quickly with the other clinics and with the hospital. Information about patient benefits and copayments needed to be quickly communicated throughout the system. Clinical information had to be rapidly relayed internally and to managed care professionals. Initially, our information systems were inadequate. We struggled with the rapid transmission of information from one part of the system to another and the adequate collection of data that were necessary to monitor the effectiveness of patient care and assist with administrative work. Time and a great deal of administrative energy ultimately brought these problems under control, but initially we felt overwhelmed.

Financial Issues. Another problem area had to do with the financial aspects of various contracts. Without much previous experience, we had to rely on data from other managed care systems. We quickly learned that there was considerable variation in data from one system to another and from one part of the country to another. As we negotiated per diem rates and capitation arrangements, we learned of the great variability in costs of mental health care. Since we were at risk with some contracts, the need to negotiate wise financial arrangements was compelling. As we began to capture utilization and cost data from within our own mental health system, we became much more adept at negotiating reasonable financial arrangements. But in the early days this was a significant problem, because the only information we could obtain was from other systems, which did not necessarily apply to the one we had created.

The Future. The Timberlawn system has now been involved in managed care contracting for five years. The system that has been put in place works much more smoothly than it did at first, but there will continue to be much fine tuning. However, the professional staff at Timberlawn now looks into the future with less anxiety and more excitement about the possibilities offered by managed care. Our initial concerns about how poorly patients might do with such brief hospital stays have been alleviated. A high percentage of patients do well with brief hospital stays that focus on rapid stabilization and discharge to outpatient services. Many patients can avoid hospital-ization altogether by utilizing intensive outpatient services. We do believe, however, that there is a small percentage of patients who need more hospital care than many managed care systems currently allow. Further data are needed to validate this conviction and to clarify the particular patient groups to which it applies.

We are working to gather data to show the effectiveness of the current treatment programs for the vast majority of our patients and the more intensive programs for others with special needs.

Overall, the movement into managed care has been very positive for Timberlawn. A professional staff with considerable managed care expertise has been developed, and we are training psychiatric residents to function well in a managed care environment. We view the future as holding new and expanded managed care opportunities for us.

DOYLE CARSON, M.D., is chief executive officer and psychiatrist-in-chief of Timberlawn Psychiatric Hospital and associate clinical professor at the University of Texas Health Science Center at Dallas.

Community-based systems of care remain the more experienced and available resources in the United States. How to adapt to the managed care enterprise will be discussed here.

Community Mental Health and Managed Care

Charles Ray, Monica Oss

The current and anticipated debate about health care reform in the United States is the most vigorous and sustained since the creation of Medicare and Medicaid. It is focused on the delivery and financing of health care and on the integration of such care into managed systems.

Ironically, this movement toward managed health and mental health in both the public and private sectors is taking place during the thirtieth anniversary of the Community Mental Health Centers (CMHC) Construction Act of 1963. The original concepts embodied in the legislation emphasized a comprehensive, integrated, and coordinated system of mental health care, provided in the least restrictive environment. It is clear that today's proposed managed behavioral health systems incorporate many of the original features and elements of the CMHC movement.

The social philosophy and values underlying the movement emphasized comprehensive community care through services for prevention, diagnosis, care, treatment, and rehabilitation. The 1960s context of social engineering was reflected in the core values of comprehensiveness, centralized services to meet all needs within a particular area, and the creation of a self-sustaining mental health system integrated over time with mainstream health care (Levy, 1986). Key elements of the original legislation included the delivery of five essential mental health services—inpatient care, outpatient care, partial hospitalization, twenty-four-hour emergency services, and consultation and education—to all without regard to age, race, religion, place of national origin, or diagnostic classification.

It was the intent of Congress that CMHCs would become self-sufficient, and the federal grants were intended as seed money. Early planners believed that while federally funded CMHCs would be required to provide a "reasonable volume" of free or reduced-cost care, fee-for-service insurance reimbursement and other third-party payments would provide a diversified funding base (Brown and Kane, 1963). It should be noted that this original design predated Medicare and Medicaid as well as the major increase in third-party indemnity coverage for behavioral health during the 1980s.

While the problems of financing CMHCs dominated the decade of the 1970s, Congress in 1976 expanded the required number of core services from five to twelve, added requirements dealing with quality assurance and cultural sensitivity, expanded CMHC governance to more closely approximate the population in the area served, and instituted multiple reporting requirements. As a result, CMHCs by the mid 1980s were dramatically different from the original concept.

These changes led to great variability among CMHCs, and they have essentially become community mental health organizations (CMHOs). Ironically, the CMHOs that pioneered many of the innovative, resource-sensitive, and clinically effective programs (such as partial hospitalization, psychosocial rehabilitation, home health care, and case management) now find that these have been adopted by private sector providers who compete with CMHOs for behavioral health benefit dollars.

Trends in Financing and Service

By 1995, analysts predict that at least 70 percent of the U.S. population will be in some type of managed care. Others suggest that this will take place even sooner. Active discussion is taking place about the roles and challenges facing CMHOs, including their ability to participate in private sector managed care. Such discussions focus on revenue diversification strategies, extension of core competencies into new markets, and protection of the social mission through the development of contemporary business-focused management styles (Broskowski and Marks, 1992).

Earlier, there appeared to be an assumption that the traditional public sector market of CMHOs was largely exempt from competition and managed care trends (Eaddy, 1992). This assumption is no longer valid, as public sector payors look to managed care programs as a means to contain costs. All this leaves traditional CMHOs poorly prepared to safeguard their share of the public market. More than thirty states have already advanced significantly toward managed care for public sector beneficiaries.

What does this mean for the current generation of CMHOs? The current trends pose a significant threat. Many proprietary managed behavioral health organizations are looking to the public sector as their next area for expansion. They propose to establish managed behavioral health programs for Medicaid and other eligible beneficiaries. Even for public officials who may be skeptical of managed care, budget crises inevitably require them to consider it.

There are several examples. Massachusetts has selected a managed behavioral health vendor to manage the mental health services for the entire Medicaid population under a full-risk capitation agreement. The Medicaid programs in Tennessee, Connecticut, and Utah already have done so. In Kansas, a consortium of CMHOs was awarded a case management contract by Medicaid to review all state-paid behavioral health services. A group in Cleveland has a capitated contract to provide child mental health services using Medicaid's 1915(a) option. The same approach is being used in Portland, Oregon. Both are Health Care Financing Administration demonstration projects.

Key Challenges

Community mental health organizations face a rapidly changing environment. Many states are now considering some form of organized or managed care, particularly for Medicaid and state employees. Providers will be caught between systems that continue to reimburse them in the old way and those that are moving toward capitated or a modified fee-for-service arrangement. This will place CMHOs under additional stress as they seek to adapt to new forms of care financing and delivery while simultaneously fulfilling their social mission.

They have, over the past few decades, operated on the assumption that their funding would be relatively stable and change relatively slowly. Their governing boards have typically been involved in stewardship issues, accounting for funds and quality of service. Board have not needed to be proactive because they operated on twelve-month budgets in which the public payors traditionally controlled both the amount and the type of services to be provided.

Now, with cost containment pressures and other payors coming into the market, boards must make complex policy decisions that balance their social missions with contemporary business practices. They need to consider access and availability of care, efficiency and productivity, financial management, their local community role, and recruiting and retaining the staff required to operate increasingly complex systems. Most nonprofit boards have not traditionally been involved in such issues.

Vermont's Experience with Managed Care

Vermont's community mental health system has, until recently, been spared the difficulty of adapting to the requirements and restrictions of managed care. Over the past few years, however, a number of national corporations' Vermont subsidiaries have contracted with managed care companies. The state itself has signed with American Biodyne to manage its employees' mental health and substance abuse benefits. As a result, the mental health centers are currently witnessing an erosion of unrestricted third-party dollars in their outpatient programs as more indemnity insurance plans become "managed." The continuation of this trend has forced centers, which wish to hold on to their outpatient business, to accept the inevitability of managed care and find ways to make it work for them.

The Vermont mental health centers were able to capitalize on their strengths as a "network" by negotiating collectively for their first major managed care contract. In 1991, American Biodyne and the Vermont Council of Community Mental Health Services worked together to come up with a general agreement that would guide individual negotiations between Biodyne and each CMHC. This approach reduced administrative time for both parties, while giving the centers greater clout than if each center had contracted independently. A major concession granted by Biodyne was the recognition of the centers as the actual providers, who in turn were given the authority to credential and approve the staff as they deemed appropriate to provide managed care services. Biodyne required tangible evidence that the centers were up to this task and requested state certification for the CMHCs participating in the contract. Another success for the centers was the rewording of what was identified as an "appropriate service" from "medically necessary" to "clinically necessary." As a result, standards of care other than a physician's (such as a psychologist's, a nurse's, or a social worker's) could be used to determine acceptable levels of treatment in a given case. This was a relevant factor in rural Vermont.

Currently, most of the CMHCs in Vermont are in the early phase of building collaborative relationships with Biodyne and other managed care companies. The impact of these partnerships has not yet been strongly felt but trends are emerging. First, the concept of partnership with a managed care company is still a new one, and both sides are still learning more about each other's corporate cultures. Managed care as a philosophy remains unfamiliar to some centers whose revenues have historically been more dependent on government subsidy than on individual consumer choice. Finally, the centers themselves are undergoing the organizational and operational changes necessary to remain viable within the increasingly competitive health care environment.

Key CMHO Management Issues

CMHO managers today face considerable challenges. Traditionally, they have been responsible for managing a fixed budget and providing services within it. They did not need to generate additional revenue or provide sophisticated marketing plans. The public sector defined who the patient or consumer would be and the rate of reimbursement. Systems were reactive and short term, focusing on cost control and quality services. Managers also were not expected to have sophisticated knowledge of different markets or of ways to provide services according to the demands of different market segments.

Now, CMHO managers have essentially three tasks: meet the institutional or organizational mission or objectives, make work productive and every worker equally achieving, and manage the social impact of work. Many of them have confused efficiency of operations with effectiveness of performance. They have focused more on cost cutting or containment than on using resources for maximum productivity. As a result, CMHOs have not used innovation in marketing as private sector managers do. Of course, the CMHO management task is complicated by the fact that there is a social mission—a public mandate to serve certain high-risk patients. CMHOs are expected to do so while diversifying to become attractive to different types of payors and consumers.

In this new environment, CMHO managers must become much more sophisticated about finance, marketing, human resources, and managing effective operations. This will not be easy because many of them are clinicians who have had little support or training in functioning as managers. They need to acquire a new set of executive skills. The traditional clinical manager is poorly prepared for systems change, team development, finance, and operating in a competitive environment.

As states all across the country move toward privatizing portions of the public mental health system, survival may become a new challenge for CMHOs. States may continue the traditional public systems in some modified form using CMHOs and other providers, or the system may be open to intense competition between private groups, CMHOs, and others. The uncertainties will lead many traditional providers to wonder how they can survive no matter the direction.

The pace of change is startling. Most CMHOs will not view these changes with a clear sense of urgency until their financing is threatened. As a result, many of them are vulnerable. They have little time left to adjust their operating systems to be accountable so that they can participate in managed care, accept at-risk financial arrangements, and develop performance and outcome measures appropriate to managed care.

What they need to do has already been well documented (Eaddy, 1992). Operational competence is highly dependent on access to critical time-sensitive data in order to manage at-risk financial contracts. While some CMHOs have had significant experience with public and private sector behavioral health demonstration projects, only a few have the infrastructure to compete successfully.

The following brief description of the Massachusetts managed care program provides an overview of certain key challenges and responses that CMHOs have made to public managed care in that state.

The Massachusetts Program

Effective July 1, 1992, Medicaid-funded behavioral health in Massachusetts began to operate under a managed care contract with a private company. The

Massachusetts decision to contain Medicaid behavioral health costs came after a legislative study found that Medicaid and welfare costs in the state had grown at an annual rate of 16 percent and had reached approximately 20 percent of the state's budget. The study recommended managed care and directed the state Medicaid agency to develop managed care programs by January 1992.

The Massachusetts Health/Managed Care Program consists of four elements: the Health Benefits Manager Program, designed to explain benefits to enrollees and to foster positive communications between primary caregivers, consumers, and providers; an HMO program; a primary care clinician program; and a mental health/substance abuse program. Under the original design, Medicaid recipients enrolled in HMOs must receive all services, including mental health and substance abuse services, through their designated HMO. A comprehensive network of primary care clinicians serves as the primary care manager for all non-HMO Medicaid recipients, who can also access mental health and substance abuse services by self-referral.

Massachusetts "carved out" mental health from physical health care and awarded the contract for management of the mental health benefits to a private company whose responsibilities include service authorization, utilization and quality management, a provider network, claims processing and payment, reporting, and interagency service coordination. During the transition, current certified Medicaid providers continue to be paid and to offer services under existing arrangements. This will change; as the programs evolve, providers will be selected at competitive rates to be included in the new smaller Medicaid provider panel.

The response of the Massachusetts CMHOs was encouraging. Their state association was proactively involved in the design of the system. Perhaps as important was the commitment of the Massachusetts CMHOs to move aggressively toward an evaluation of their organizational readiness to participate in managed care systems as well as to ascertain what elements of their current service mix would be most applicable to the new environment.

While it is still quite early, the experience of the Massachusetts CMHOs so far suggests that while CMHOs may surrender their long-held, sole service "franchise" for the public sector, they are able to move effectively and with reasonable speed to participate in the new systems. Strategic alliances with primary care clinicians, mergers and affiliations between CMHOs and health care facilities, and the development of new services more appropriate to managed care are all being pursued. The familiarity of CMHOs with the high-risk Medicaid population also gives them an important advantage.

What CMHOs Should Do Now

CMHOs are now at a critical juncture in their history. They must compete in the evolving national health system and demonstrate that they are efficient providers with clear value. CMHOs will find that survival is extremely diffi-cult without well-developed marketing strategies, and they must continue to serve high-risk, long-term patients while extending their roles in acute and intermediate managed care.

They will also have to thoroughly evaluate their internal resources, products, and services to become more effective. CMHOs, even relatively large ones, are often small in comparison with mainstream health care orga-nizations. They often suffer from lack of capital, obsolescent infrastructures, and a confusing array of mandates, identities, and visions. At present, their options appear to be as follows:

Maintain the status quo. Certain highly rural and remote geographic areas may be exempt from severe changes, as will their CMHOs. A status quo strategy will still require them to gauge whether or not they will be able to survive in capitated reimbursement systems and whether they are truly im-mune to changes or new competitors.

Promote merger or affiliation. Drawbacks for traditional stand-alone CMHOs include their relative isolation from mainstream primary health care and difficulty in obtaining capital for new facilities. There has been a recent noticeable increase in merger and affiliation activities between acute care hospitals and more entrepreneurial CMHOs. It seems clear that the develop-ment of regional and national vertically integrated systems of care makes iso-lated CMHOs vulnerable to losing their referral networks. Considerations of affiliation or merger should be based on such factors as commonly shared values, the ability to derive economies of scale through the reduction of du-plicate overhead or administrative services, potential for increased market share, and appropriate ways to reduce competition. CMHOs may be attrac-tive to larger health care organizations because they have a demonstrated ability to provide effective non-facility-based care and are already established in their communities.

Offer new services. CMHOs may also experiment with new market niches focusing on their ability to provide either a competitive low-cost or a value-added approach to behavioral health. Many CMHOs are adding basic behavioral health services aimed at self-pay consumers in addition to third-party reimbursement. Affiliations as providers with managed care entities offer short-term approaches toward gaining experience and competence, as well as a reputation for being effective. Developing competencies in such new areas as workers' compensation and disability can be helpful. The tradi-tional strengths of CMHOs—case management, prevention, wellness, and ambulatory, residential, or partial-care services—may have a new and excit-ing worth in the evolving managed care market. CMHOs may also continue to play important roles in prevention, wellness, and the provision of em-ployee assistance program services. In addition, by virtue of their familiarity with judicial and correctional institutions, CMHOs may have an important edge in the development of new and specialized programs for these areas.

Whatever strategies CMHOs select, it is clear that the transition will not be easy. By the mid 1990s, it will not matter whether CMHOs view their markets as public or private sector; the providers that survive will be practicing in a remarkably similar manner. Survivors will be efficient provider organizations that can live with prospective or capitated systems while offering quality services with demonstrated outcomes and benefits.

Threats and Opportunities

In the future, all third-party payments from public and private payors will be through participation in managed care only. Traditional fee-for-service arrangements will, for all practical purposes, vanish in this decade. CMHOs must be able to participate in new reimbursement systems focusing on partial or full risk sharing. They must develop clinical, operational, and financial systems that allow them to monitor, measure, and communicate their performance. Electronic information exchange is integral to these tasks.

Behavioral health providers will find the distinctions between "managed care" and "providers" fading dramatically in the future. Provider organizations will be developing managed care competencies, which in effect will make them "mini-managed clinical organizations." Once providers are paid on an "at-risk" basis, they have even more at stake than external third-party management entities in living within their resource limits. If this trend continues, the future behavioral health delivery system will be dominated by hybrid entities and networks that are at the same time both provider and insurer. Traditional CMHOs have had long experience living with limited resources. However, they have had less experience in the development and operation of sophisticated clinical and financial arrangements or participating in organized networks beyond their traditional catchment areas.

One of the potentially most important changes for CMHOs is the shift from payment based on location of service to payment based on outcome and performance. The initial evidence of this trend is the declining census of inpatient psychiatric and chemical dependency treatment programs, as care formerly provided in those settings is moved to less resource-intensive and more clinically effective ones. However, the impact of non-fee-for-service payment methods will move beyond inpatient settings to outpatient settings as well. The development of home health care, mobile and responsive crisis services, and team use of new psychoeducational, brief focused achievement, and care management approaches will allow more flexible care. The driving force behind these programs will be their lower cost for similar performance results. Both providers and payors will need to look beyond traditional definitions of care to succeed in this evolving delivery system. With their ability to offer innovative and less costly approaches, CMHOs hold strong promise in this area.

Provider Marketing Strategies

Managed behavioral health programs affect the way providers are paid and how patients get to them. Both of these should have a significant effect on provider marketing strategies. Traditionally, the financing of most behavioral health benefits was through fee-for-service payments by third-party payors. With managed care programs, payment for services is moving away from fee-for-service and toward risk-based payments, either per-case fees or capitation payments. These risk-based payments are often linked to performance.

The growing dominance of managed behavioral health programs also affects how patients select providers. Under traditional fee-for-service arrangements with third-party payors, providers were free to communicate directly to patients. Patients were free to select the provider of their choice. Under most managed care plans, a patient's ability to select a provider ranges from conditional to nonexistent (exclusive provider arrangements). In this situation, the provider has several customers: the patient, the patient's family, the referral source, and the managed care program.

Given these changes, provider marketing strategies look quite different from those of just a few years ago. In evaluating new marketing strategies, providers must consider four elements—product lines, pricing, promotion, and distribution. From a strategy perspective, managed care programs have become the new distribution system for behavioral health services. Product lines, pricing, and promotion strategies must be altered with this in mind.

Providers in the private sector have made significant changes in the structure of their programs and their marketing activities to stay competitive in this changing market. Some have established their own managed care divisions to provide complete patient care on an insured or per-case basis. A number of them have established preferred provider organizations that contract directly with payors for mental health and chemical dependency services. Other provider groups have established structured outpatient programs that insurers can use in lieu of traditional inpatient treatment.

Summary

CMHOs are the heirs to a rich tradition of coordinated and comprehensive services and appropriate clinical outcomes in the least restrictive settings. The early CMHO focus on prevention, coordination of services, continuity of care, and partial and residential services, as well as psychosocial and case management methodologies, underlies contemporary managed behavioral health programs. This provides CMHOs with a great opportunity to be major participants in the new programs.

References

Browkowski, A., and Marks, E. *Managed Mental Healthcare: Innovations in Community Mental Health.* Sarasota, Fla.: Professional Resource Press, 1992.

Brown, B., and Kane, H. P. "The Many Meanings of Comprehensive: Underlying Issues in Implementing the Community Mental Health Program." *American Journal of Orthopsychiatry,* 1963, *34* (5), 834–839.

Eaddy, M. L. *The Private Community Mental Health Organization in Innovations in Community Mental Health.* Sarasota, Fla.: Professional Resource Press, 1992.

Levy, L. "Financing Organization and Control: The Problem of Implementing Comprehensive Community Mental Health Sentences." *American Journal of Public Health,* 1969, *59* (1), 40–47.

CHARLES RAY, M.Ed., *is chief executive officer of the National Council of Community Mental Health Centers.*

MONICA OSS, M.A., *teaches at Johns Hopkins University. She is editor and publisher of* Open Minds *newsletter and a consultant to private and public organizations in designing new approaches to the managed care environment.*

Substance abuse by the late 1980s had already become a prominent, out-of-control sector of health care. Some of the reasons for this crisis, as well as more recent changes in this specialty field, are explicated in this chapter.

Substance Abuse and Managed Care

Claire V. Wilson

Substance abuse continues to be a major American public health problem "accounting for over $2.4 billion in treatment and prevention expenditures in 1989" (Wheeler, Fadel, and D'Aunno, 1992). But it has a recovery rate and a more favorable treatment outcome than other potentially life-threatening illnesses. If left untreated, however, as with other progressive relapsing illnesses, the outcome is potentially lethal. In contrast to the situation with other chronic medical illnesses—for example, diabetes mellitus or hypertension—private health insurance benefits for substance abuse either do not exist or are discriminatory. This contradicts the fact that effective treatment for substance abuse problems lowers medical/surgical expenses.

It is doubted, however, if more expensive inpatient treatments provide additional short- and long-term benefits sufficient to offset their greater cost. The skyrocketing utilization and costs of substance abuse treatment during the last ten years have alarmed corporate benefit managers. Its subjective and therefore suspicious nature, combined with high costs, raised questions about the value of substance abuse benefits. Hence, one major factor in the advent of managed behavioral health care comes into focus.

Increased Cost and Utilization

Increased utilization is attributable to a variety of factors: decreased stigma associated with seeking treatment, increases in the incidence of substance abuse in an employed population coping with economic stress, and increased publicity and provider exploitation of available benefits. The sunsetting (expiration) of certificate-of-need legislation in many states, followed by aggressive marketing aimed at potential patients, caused what had been the second-class citizens of health care—psychiatry and substance abuse—to become lucrative services. Corporate America paid for benefit designs that favored inpatient care; based on the notion that unlimited freedom of choice and access must be maintained to preserve quality of care, it helped fuel the rise of the proprietary psychiatric hospital industry.

Hospitals established local outpatient centers, often as feeders to hospitalization. In substance abuse, detoxification units and outpatient programs were also frequently linked with adult rehabilitation programs in a direct feeder relationship. Due to the incentives for the use of high-cost inpatient services during this high-growth phase of the psychiatric hospital industry, substance abuse, when not covered, was misdiagnosed and mistreated—frequently as depression. Cocaine dependence, for example, was often diagnosed as major depression and treated in a freestanding psychiatric hospital for thirty days, often exhausting the patient's behavioral health benefits. Admissions to private psychiatric hospitals for treatment of substance abuse increased by 64 percent between 1980 and 1986. Large unexpected treatment costs related to adolescents were noted with increasing frequency.

While individualized treatment was marketed, it was not delivered, and there was a lack of accountability in terms of treatment outcome. Expensive inpatient programs provided every patient with the same "individualized treatment" whether or not they needed it, using a regressive "3R" model of treatment—remove from society, repair the problem, and replace in society.

When a major insurance carrier first paid for a twenty-eight-day residential, nonhospital alcohol treatment in 1972, the twenty-eight-day length of stay became a clinical commandment. It was not based on empirical data. The average patient in the late 1960s and 1970s at the "Minnesota model" alcohol abstinence-based residential treatment programs was a white, heterosexual, employed, married male who was dependent on alcohol (Anderson, 1981; Laundergan, 1982). These programs were designed by middle-class, white males influenced by the traditions and twelve-step programs of Alcoholics Anonymous (AA). It was also white, middle-class males that seemed to do well in AA-type self-support groups (Rawson, 1990). Today's patient mix is different, as are the drugs of choice.

Many corporate benefit managers concluded that these practices and the dramatic utilization increases that resulted from them were induced by treatment providers who exploited the benefits available. Suspicion was highest for proprietary psychiatric and substance abuse inpatient facilities (Dixon, 1992).

Managed Care

Employers and other payors became dissatisfied and disillusioned with a perceived waste of resources and lack of discernible value. Dramatic rises in utilization were believed to be driven by the fee-for-service, utilization maximization strategies of providers. Employee assistance programs (EAPs) were proliferating as treatment costs escalated but were not seen as effective in containing costs.

As a result, employers came to demand rational benefit and cost management as well as provider accountability for honest clinical communication and documented quality service (Nassef, 1992). Many decided to choose managed care as the solution rather than eliminating or reducing benefits.

Managed behavioral health care is broadly defined operationally by Goodman, Brown, and Deitz (1992, p. 5) as "any patient care that is not determined solely by the provider." The externally imposed review or examination of treatment by case managers was especially disconcerting to an ideologically oriented field that had few specific treatment standards, much less an internal review process (Weedman, 1992), and dogmatic insistence on fixed lengths of stay. Inpatient programs were essentially based on one treatment model for all different types of patients, problems, and circumstances.

Professionally managed behavioral health companies were the first to expect providers to be open to accountability for individualized diagnoses and treatment. The challenge to the hospital-based providers was to justify the necessity and appropriateness of care based on careful assessment, problem identification, and goal-focused treatment planning. This interaction began to resculpt the rigid delivery system.

Ethical managed care demands not immediate expense reduction but rational patient placement decisions based on vertically integrated provider networks that can deliver all levels and dimensions of care. Flexibility in treatment planning and patient movement along a continuum of care that is case managed by a trained, licensed professional should be hallmarks of good managed behavioral health care. In the new era of managed care, substance abuse treatment became an early area of scrutiny.

Chemical Dependency Case Example

A case example will illustrate many of the above points.

> The patient is a thirty-nine-year-old man who is employed as a regional sales manager for a cellular telephone company in a major American city. He has been separated from his wife for the past seven months, citing financial "stress" as a cause of the marital conflict. He has a pending driving-under-the-influence (DUI) charge and is afraid of a conviction, which could result in suspension of his driver's license.
>
> He referred himself to his EAP for "marriage counseling" but admits to drinking bouts that are becoming more frequent since his wife left him. The couple has an eleven-year-old son, who is living with his mother. The patient visits his son one day every weekend. However, the patient failed to pick his son up last weekend, since he was too hung over from an all-night outing with ex-army buddies.

During his EAP evaluation, the patient also admitted to snorting and smoking cocaine on the weekend, adding that he feels lonely and sad. He describes isolating himself and overworking during the week but drinking alcohol and using cocaine in a binge pattern on weekends with peers who are also heavy consumers of psychoactive substances.

When pressed about the financial stress, the patient described "living from paycheck to paycheck" and then further disclosed that he was pursuing loans because he was falling behind on paying his bills. When pressed further, he admitted to spending approximately $300 to $500 a week on alcohol and cocaine.

The patient denied any psychiatric history in himself or primary relatives. He denied any suicidal intention, plan, or history of previous attempts. He did admit to feelings of helplessness and hopelessness at times. He described both his father and his paternal grandfather as "heavy drinkers." He takes medication on an as-needed basis for his asthma. He denied any signs or symptoms of alcohol withdrawal. He did complain of insomnia and loss of appetite.

The patient was concerned about his employer finding out about his DUI charges and possible consequences in the workplace. He was seeking EAP advice on how to deal with the charges as well.

Through his employer group, his chemical dependency benefit was one course of inpatient treatment per year and a maximum of two courses of treatment over a lifetime, with up to thirty days per admission. The thirty-day limit included detoxification and aftercare services. Besides the thirty-day limit, there was a $10,000 benefit per course of treatment in the provider network or $5,000 maximum per course of treatment out of the preferred provider network. The employer group EAP could arrange for assessment and referral but had no authority to review or reimburse treatment services.

Before Managed Care. The employee was referred by his EAP counselor to a traditional twenty-eight-day inpatient nonhospital or residential alcohol rehabilitation program about one hundred miles from the patient's home. The counselor recommended this program at the patient's request and agreed that it was in the patient's best interest to be out of the area for a while, away from the temptations of "people, places, and things." The patient was encouraged to use a combination of paid vacation time and unpaid leave of absence from work. The cost of this program was $8,400, not including aftercare services. The counselor further recommended that the patient complete this rehabilitation course before his DUI hearing as a strategy that might serve the patient well in court. The patient agreed and was able to utilize the program to establish and maintain abstinence. However, three months later, after successfully completing traffic school, the patient relapsed after his wife filed for divorce. She was not impressed by his completion of the rehabilitation program. The patient never really complied with attending self-help support groups in his community or outpatient aftercare arrangements the program made. Since the patient never attended self-support groups in his own community, he was unfamiliar with the variety of meetings where he might feel more comfortable and used his work schedule as an excuse to avoid attending them. Also, he felt no real connection to the outpatient counseling program. The aftercare arrangements were too much of an abrupt transition for this patient, who began to describe the purpose of his previous treatment as to teach him to control his use. Now threatened with disciplinary action at work for absenteeism in a Friday-Monday pattern, the patient sought an intensive outpatient treatment program in his community. Since he had only $1,600 left of his benefit for that year, he had to pay an additional $2,400 out of his own pocket. This was disposable income that he did not have due to his cocaine use.

After Managed Care. After receiving a careful assessment on an outpatient basis by a licensed professional familiar with the diagnosis and treatment of addictive disease, the patient was referred to an intensive outpatient treatment program in his own community. The cost of this program for a full year of treatment, including aftercare services, was $4,000, with $6,000 of benefit remaining in case of serious relapse. During the first six weeks of the program, the patient was connected with self-help support groups and a temporary sponsor in his own community. During the intensive phase of treatment, he attended daily sessions during the week, after work. On weekends he was required to attend self-help support meetings. The patient was able to again establish and maintain abstinence, as demonstrated by urine surveillance. During the less intensive phases of treatment, he attended individual sessions on an as-needed basis and group sessions weekly while continuing to heavily utilize self-help support. While he experienced lapses at three months and six months, he was quickly able to reestablish abstinence. After nine months, family therapy was begun with his wife and son. The patient will continue to be followed and monitored by both the treatment provider and the managed care company for the next two years. The patient did not have to utilize any vacation time or unpaid leave to participate in his treatment. This was especially important at a time when there were a variety of economic and psychosocial stressors.

Stresses and Strains

Providers of acute inpatient and residential drug and alcohol treatment tended to view managed care in any of its manifestations more as an adversary than an ally, failing to recognize their role in its development. Entrenched ideological allegiance rather than critical self-examination within the substance abuse treatment industry and some EAPs set the stage for turf battles over what constituted appropriate, necessary treatment. Rawson and others (1989) have described how during the last half of the 1980s, the dramatic increase in intensive outpatient programs for the treatment of drug and alcohol problems paralleled the rapid development of the managed behavioral health industry. Substance abuse outpatient treatment programs and managed behavioral health, as the designated agent of the payor, formed an alliance, the potential of which has not yet been fully realized. Despite the promise of an efficacious model that was at least comparable to inpatient care for the appropriately matched patient yet considerably less expensive, referral volumes were slow to materialize. The lag in referrals contributed to the unfortunate fallout of early innovators in alternative ambulatory services.

Since payors, not patients or providers, stimulated the evolution of managed care, the two latter constituencies do not always understand its components or the new service systems that are influencing them. The early managed care models for behavioral health were derived from managed medical care—particularly utilization management—of which the substance abuse treatment industry was largely unaware. Before managed care, medical services, especially hospital care, were provided and then paid for after the care was delivered. This type of payment (retrospective reimbursement) failed to influence provider behavior with regard to costs and contributed to the development of prospective payment.

The Future

In the 1990s, a way to resolve the lingering conflicts between providers and care managers is a more professional collaboration, including agreement that substance abuse is a disease requiring a family orientation and that the use of empirically derived patient placement criteria can provide a basis for common understanding and practice (American Society of Addiction Medicine, 1991). A standardized intake, assessment, and outcome methodology to determine addiction severity (Furman, Prikh, Bragg, and McLellan, 1990) has been put forth and widely endorsed by providers and case managers. The American Society of Addiction Management's (ASAM) six dimensions examine the characteristics of patients' problems and recommend levels of care and appropriate resources. The ASAM approach is a systematized way of making accurate, specific patient placement decisions that are predictable, reviewable, affordable, and efficacious. This helps to reduce the clinical versus financial issue and can reassure provider, patient, and payor that costs are being contained. Basic decisions are made as to levels and dimensions of care according to the need for medical management; the structure, safety, and security needs of an individual patient; and the intensity of treatment required according to severity. An unplanned consequence of managed mental health care has been the acceleration of addiction medicine as an accredited medical subspecialty.

Another remaining major area of controversy in the inpatient versus outpatient placement argument is the "fail first" philosophy, or access restrictions used by managed care entities that seem more financially than clinically driven. This approach requires that a patient fail first at the least restrictive level of care, usually outpatient, before any other treatment is authorized. This orientation repeats the nonclinical, one-way-for-all error that critics of the routine twenty-eight-day hospital stay have pointed to.

While this potentially dangerous philosophy may lead to short-term profits for some managed behavioral health firms, it is not meeting the needs of anyone else. The long-term costly result can be deterioration and revolving-door outpatient treatment for substance abuse problems.

The ASAM patient placement criteria, with their crosswalk of levels and dimensions of care based on DSM-III-R diagnosis of substance use disorders, represents an important beginning toward establishing a clinically oriented, level playing field for patients, treatment providers, care managers, employer groups, insurance companies, and government. With collaboration between EAPs, managed care companies, and substance abuse providers not only to control costs but to place patients rationally, effectively, and safely, great progress can be made.

Managed behavioral health care has challenged substance abuse treatment providers to examine and creatively change their orientations and practices. In the 1990s, corporate and public payors will accept no less.

References

American Society of Addiction Medicine. *ASAM Patient Placement Criteria for the Treatment of Psychoactive Substance Use Disorders.* Washington, D.C.: American Society of Addiction Medicine, 1991.

Anderson, D. *Perspectives on Treatment: The Minnesota Experience.* Center City, Minn.: Hazelden Foundation, 1981.

Dixon, K. "Mental Health: Can EAP's and Managed Care Cooperate?" *Journal of Health Care Benefits,* 1992, 2 (2), 28–33.

Furman, B., Prikh, G., Bragg, A., and McLellan, T. *Addiction Severity Index.* (5th ed.) Philadelphia: University of Pennsylvania/Veterans Administration Center for Studies of Addiction, 1990.

Goodman, M., Brown, J., and Deitz, P. *Managing Managed Care: A Mental Health Practitioner's Survival Guide.* Washington, D.C.: American Psychiatric Press, 1992.

Laundergan, J. *Easy Does It: Alcoholism Treatment Outcomes.* Center City, Minn.: Hazelden Foundation, 1982.

Nassef, D. "A Payor Sounds Off About the Treatment Industry." *Addiction and Recovery,* 1992, 12 (3), 17.

Rawson, R. "Cut the Crack: The Policy Maker's Guide to Cocaine Treatment." *Policy Review,* 1990, 10 (Winter), 10–19.

Rawson, R., Obert, J., McCann, M., Smith, D., and Ling, W. *Neurobehavioral Treatment for Cocaine Dependency: Relapse Prevention Programming.* Newbury Park, Calif.: Sage, 1989.

Weedman, R. "Fundamentals of Communication." *Addiction and Recovery,* 1992, 12 (3), 18–21.

Wheeler, J., Fadel, H., and D'Aunno, T. "Ownership and Performance of Outpatient Substance Abuse Treatment Centers." *American Journal of Public Health,* 1992, 82, 711–717.

CLAIRE V. WILSON, Ph.D., is vice president of development at Mustard Seed, Inc., assistant clinical professor of psychology at University of California, Los Angeles, and former regional clinical director for Southern California at U.S. Behavioral Health.

INDEX

Adolescents: Alcan Aluminum health plan for, 62, 63; managed health care for, 13–26; in Medicaid population, 69

Affective psychoses, 31

Alcan Aluminum health plan, 55–65; background, 56–58; benefit objectives, 56; carve-out decision, 58–61; clinical referral line, 63; consensus building, 64; credentialing of practitioners, 62–63; customer service requirements, 63; design of MHSA program, 61–64; diagram of plan design, 61; employee assistance programs, 56, 58, 59, 61; implementation of, 64; integrated EAP/managed care program, 62; 1990–1991 inpatient services, 59; paid claims experience, 58; point-of-service plan design of, 60; provider access, 63; quality assurance program, 63–64; self-funding of, 56; USBH and, 59, 61

Alcohol abuse. See Substance abuse

Alcoholics Anonymous (AA), 100

American Biodyne, 91–92

American Society of Addiction Medicine (ASAM), 104–105

Anderson, D., 100

Anderson, J. P., 43

Angel, K., 10

Aukerman, G.F., 41

Biofeedback, 32

Bird, H. R., 49

Blose, J. O., 27, 35

Boyle, M. H., 49

Bragg, A., 104

Briefer therapies: brief-therapy adult developmental model, 29; provider perspective on, 83

Broskowski, A., 7, 41, 90

Brown, B., 90

Brown, J., 101

Callahan, D., 41, 42

Capitation, 1

Care managers, 8–9; under Alcan Aluminum health plan, 63; children and adolescents, role with, 15–17; CMHOs and, 90; in Massachusetts health program, 94; in USBH model, 18

Certificate-of-need legislation, sunsetting of, 99–100

Chemical dependency. See Substance abuse

Children: managed health care for, 13–26; in Medicaid population, 69

Chronic medical diagnosis (CMD) group in Hawaii Medicaid project, 35–37

CMHOs. See Community mental health organizations.

Cocaine dependence. See Substance abuse

Community mental health, 89–90

Community Mental Health Centers (CMHC) Construction Act of 1963, 89–90

Community mental health organizations (CMHOs), 90–98; challenges to, 91; financing trends, 90–91; future of, 94–96; management issues, 92–93; in Massachusetts, 93–94; new services of, 95; provider marketing strategies for, 97; in Vermont, 91–92

Connecticut, managed care in, 91

Costello, E. J., 49

Cost-offset effect, 27–40; outpatient mental health services and, 28

Cotton, P., 42, 43

Cronin, C., 5

Daniels, N., 42, 43

D'Aunno, T., 99

Deitz, P., 101

Department of Transportation, 58

Depression: in Hawaii Medicaid project, 32; outcome modules for, 10

DHHS. See U.S. Department of Health and Human Services

Diabetes, 28

Diagnoses: accuracy in, 7; chronic medical diagnosis, 35–37; in Hawaii Medicaid project, 31–32

Diagnostic related group (DRG) payment method, 70

Digital Equipment Corporation's OSC, 10

Dixon, K., 100

107

McLellan, T., 104
Malpractice: Oregon Health Plan and, 42
Managed care, 1; Alcan Aluminum health plan, 55–65; beginnings of, 82–83; community mental health and, 89–90; in Connecticut, 91; in Massachusetts, 93–94; Medicaid research project on, 27–40; in Ohio, 91; provider perspective on, 81–87; in public sector, 67–80; substance abuse and, 99–105; Timberlawn Psychiatric Hospital program, 84–87; in Vermont, 91–92. *See also* Organized systems of care
Managed competition, 1
Managed Mental Healthcare Association, 10
Marketing CMHOs, 93
Marks, E., 90
Massachusetts, managed care in, 91, 93–94
Massachusetts Health/Managed Care Program, 94
Mechcatie, E., 46
Medicaid: children and adolescents covered by, 69; and community mental health centers, 90; implications of managed mental health treatment, 39; institutions for mental disease, 72; and managed care in Massachusetts, 93–94; Oregon Health Plan and, 41, 52. *See also* Hawaii Medicaid project; Valley Mental Health
Medicare and community mental health centers, 90
Mental health and substance abuse (MHSA) care: Alcan Aluminum plan, 55, 57
Mental health carve-out, 55
Mergers of CMHOs, 95
Mild to moderate disturbance in USBH model, 25–26
Minnesota model for residential treatment, 100
Moderate disturbance in USBH model, 24–25
Moderate to moderately severe disturbance in USBH model, 22–24
Moran, M., 41, 46
Mumford, E., 27, 28, 35

Nassef, D., 101
National Center for Health Services Research, 6–7
Nerenz, D. R., 42, 46
Network-based case management, 2
Non-CMD group in Hawaii Medicaid project, 35–37
Non–network-based utilization review, 1–2

Offord, D. R., 49
Ohio, managed care in, 91
Ontario Health Study, 49
Open hospital units, 15
Oregon Health Plan, 41–54, 91; actuarial estimates for, 45; criteria for condition-treatment pairs, 44; defining basic health care in, 42; examples of medical/surgical condition-treatment pairs, 51; financing of, 42, 52; future of, 51–52; implementation of, 49–50, 52; integration of physical and mental health, 50–51; mental health and chemical dependency provisions, 46–47; priorities in health service, 43; ranking list under, 48–49; revision of condition-treatment categories, 43–45; triage in, 50
Oregon Health Services Commission, 42, 44
Oregon Psychiatric Association, 43, 49
Organized systems of care (OSCs), 5–6; characteristics of, 8–9; cost increases, 6; Digital Equipment Corporation's, 10; differences from current managed care, 8; Honeywell's OSC, 9–10; transition to, 11
Outcome modules, 10–11
Outcomes Management Consortium, 10
Outpatient care, 15; brief-therapy adult developmental model, 29

Panic disorder, 10
Parents, involvement of, 14
Partial hospitalization, 15, 90
Personality disorders, 51
Pharmacotherapy in Oregon Health Plan, 47
Precertification by Valley Mental Health, 77
Prikh, G., 104

ORDERING INFORMATION

NEW DIRECTIONS FOR MENTAL HEALTH SERVICES is a series of paperback books that presents timely and readable volumes on subjects of concern to clinicians, administrators, and others involved in the care of the mentally disabled. Each volume is devoted to one topic and includes a broad range of authoritative articles written by noted specialists in the field. Books in the series are published quarterly in spring, summer, fall, and winter and are available for purchase by subscription and individually.

SUBSCRIPTIONS for 1993 cost $54.00 for individuals (a savings of 25 percent over single-copy prices) and $75.00 for institutions, agencies, and libraries. Please do not send institutional checks for personal subscriptions. Standing orders are accepted.

SINGLE COPIES cost $17.95 when payment accompanies order. (California, New Jersey, New York, and Washington, D.C., residents please include appropriate sales tax.) Billed orders will be charged postage and handling.

DISCOUNTS for quantity orders are available. Please write to the address below for information.

ALL ORDERS must include either the name of an individual or an official purchase order number. Please submit your order as follows:
   Subscriptions: specify series and year subscription is to begin
   Single copies: include individual title code (such as MHS58)

MAIL ALL ORDERS TO:
   Jossey-Bass Publishers
   350 Sansome Street
   San Francisco, California 94104

FOR SINGLE-COPY SALES OUTSIDE OF THE UNITED STATES CONTACT:
   Maxwell Macmillan International Publishing Group
   866 Third Avenue
   New York, New York 10022

FOR SUBSCRIPTION SALES OUTSIDE OF THE UNITED STATES, contact any international subscription agency or Jossey-Bass directly.